The Complete

Diabetic Cookbook

For Beginners

Transforming Diabetic Diets | 30 Days Meal Plan

To Manage Type 2 Diabetes, Newly Diagnosed, and

Prediabetes with Delicious and Super Easy and Healthy Recipes

By EMILY KEMP

2023 Edition

DISCLAIMER

The book "*The Complete Diabetic Cookbook for Beginners*" aims to provide accurate and reliable information on the topic discussed. However, readers need to understand that the publisher is not responsible for providing accounting, legal, or other specialized services related to publishing.

While every effort has been made to ensure the accuracy of the information presented, the reader assumes all hazards linked with the use or misuse of any policies, practices, or guidelines mentioned in the book, whether due to carelessness or any other reason. The author cannot be held liable for any direct or indirect financial or other losses that may occur because of using the information provided.

As of 2023, all rights to the eBook are protected by copyright. Without the author's complete and signed written permission, the information may not be copied, recorded, or transmitted electronically or mechanically. Respect for the author's intellectual property rights is appreciated.

TABLE OF CONTENTS

Introduction..9

Chapter 1...12

UNDERSTANDING DIABETES...12

    What is Diabetes?..12

    Symptoms of Diabetes..13

    Causes of Diabetes...13

    Diagnosing and Monitoring Diabetes..14

    Stages of Diabetes..15

Chapter 2...17

EXPLORING DIFFERENT FORMS OF DIABETES..................................17

    Type 1 Diabetes..17

    Type 2 Diabetes..18

    Gestational Diabetes...19

    Other Less Common Types of Diabetes...20

    Unique Characteristics And Management Approaches..........................20

Chapter 3...23

DIABETIC DIET...23

    Recommended Foods in Diabetic Diet..23

    Benefits of a Diabetic Diet...24

    Creating a Diabetic-Friendly Meal Plan..24

    Other Considerations for Diabetic Diet...24

Chapter 4...27

WHAT TO EXPECT IN THIS COOKBOOK?..27

Chapter 5...31

BREAKFAST..31

1. Banana Pancakes 32

2. Asparagus Frittata 32

3. Cauliflower Scramble 33

4. Stuffed Tomatoes 33

5. Mushroom Omelette 34

6. Blueberry Pancakes 34

7. Cheesy Scrambled Eggs 36

8. Almond Berry Oatmeal 36

9. Pumpkin Spice Muffins 37

10. Seedy Muesli 37

11. Healthy Granola 38

12. Multigrain Avocado Toast 38

Chapter 6 .... **40**

SOUPS & STEWS **40**

1. Mexican Tortilla Soup 41

2. Turkey & Rice Soup 41

3. Tasty Tomato Soup 42

4. Creamy Mushroom Soup 42

5. Minestrone with Parmigiano Reggiano 43

6. Pumpkin Soup 43

7. White Bean Soup 44

8. Creamy Broccoli Soup 44

9. Butternut Squash Soup 45

10. Lentil Soup 45

Chapter 7 .... **48**

Poultry **48**

1. Lemon Chicken Breast 49

2. Chicken Nuggets 49

3. Shredded Buffalo Chicken 50

4. Crispy Chicken Thighs 50

5. Chicken Masala 51

6. Thanksgiving Turkey Breast 51

7. Chicken Pot Pie 52

8. Turkey and Quinoa Caprese Casserole 52

9. Lemon-Pepper Chicken Wings 53

10. Teriyaki Turkey Meatballs 53

11. Baked Spaghetti with Ground Turkey 54

Chapter 8 56

BEEF & PORK 56

1. Bavarian Beef 57

2. Pork Chop Diane 57

3. Beef Stroganoff 58

4. Sage-Parmesan Pork Chops 58

5. Black Bean and Beef Steak Tacos 59

6. Cheddar-Beef Burger 59

7. Steak Gyro Platter 60

8. Grilled Pork Loin Chops 60

9. Mustard Herb Pork Tenderloin 61

10. Jalapeno Popper Pork Chops 61

Chapter 9 64

FISH & SEAFOOD 64

1. Seafood Risotto 65

2. Trout with Basil Sauce 65

3. Caprese Shrimp Pasta 66

4. COD with Mango Salsa 66

5. Sole Piccata 67

6. Catfish with Corn and Pepper Relish 67

7. Blackened Salmon 68

8. Aromatic Mackerel 68

9. Tuna Poke with Riced Broccoli 69

10. Baked Cod with Tomatoes and Olives 69

Chapter 10 72

VEGETABLES AND SIDE DISHES 72

1. Apple-Carrot Salad 73

2. Feta Spinach Salad 73

3. Easy Mashed Cauliflower 74

4. Chickpeas with Spinach 74

5. Heirloom Tomato Salad 75

6. Broccoli Salad 75

7. Lemon-Garlic Mushrooms 76

8. Zucchini Saute 76

9. Broccoli with Pine Nuts 77

10. Fennel and Chickpeas 77

Chapter 11 80

SNACKS AND APPERTIZERS 80

1. Parmesan Zucchini Fries 81

2. Tuna Ceviche 81

3. Open Sardine Sandwich 82

4. Hummus 82

5. Fresh Dill Dip 83

6. Creamy Cheese Dip 83

7. Spinach and Artichoke Dip 84

8. No-Bake Coconut and Cashew Energy Bars 84

9. Cinnamon Toasted Pumpkin Seeds 85

10. Cucumber Pate 85

Chapter 12 88

DESSERTS 88

1. Fried Apples 89

2. Strawberry Cream Cheese Crepes 89

3. Raspberry Nice Cream 90

4. Cherry Almond Cobbler 90

5. Basic Pie Crust 91

6. Crustless Peanut Butter Cheesecake 91

7. Lemon Dessert Shots 92

8. Chocolate Cupcakes 92

9. Pumpkin Spice Waffles 93

10. Blueberry Yogurt Cake 93

ndex: 30-Day Meal Plan 95

Conclusion 98

ABOUT AUTHOR

EMILY KEMP is an experienced and passionate nutritionist with a profound dedication to helping individuals lead healthier lives while managing diabetes. Emily's interest in nutrition sparked during her early adulthood when she witnessed her close family members facing the challenges of diabetes.

Enthusiastic about cooking since her childhood, Emily combined her culinary talents with her expertise in nutrition to create a collection of delicious and diabetes-friendly recipes. Her goal is to inspire and motivate individuals to take charge of their diabetes management with confidence and enthusiasm.

Emily Kemp's mission is to transform the way we approach diabetic nutrition. With her expertise and compassionate guidance, you will discover the joy of wholesome eating, empowering you to lead a vibrant life while effectively managing diabetes.

Together, let us embrace a healthier and happier future!

One delicious recipe at a time.!

****

INTRODUCTION

Laughter is often called the best medicine. Well, for people with diabetes, insulin becomes your superhero!

Hungry for mouthwatering meals that will not spike your blood sugar?

In today's world, managing diabetes is more crucial than ever, with an increasing number of people being diagnosed with this condition. Whether you are newly diagnosed or seeking comprehensive information and practical guidance on diabetes management, this book is here to be your invaluable resource.

Our goal is to provide a solid understanding of diabetes, including its causes, symptoms, and impact on your body. With this knowledge, you will be better equipped to drive informed decisions for your lifestyle, diet, and treatment options.

This guide is designed to cater to all types of diabetes, whether type 1, type 2, gestational diabetes, or less common forms. You will find tailored insights and management approaches for each type, helping you navigate your journey toward improved health.

We understand the significance of convenience and simplicity in your daily life. That is why we've included a collection of healthy and easy-to-follow recipes to make cooking enjoyable and stress-free. Our cookbook section contains delicious recipes specially crafted for people with diabetes. These recipes are tasty and carefully designed to help you manage your blood sugar levels while savoring the pleasure of tasty food.

But managing diabetes goes beyond just dietary adjustments.

It requires a holistic approach that includes lifestyle modifications and regular exercise. That is why we go beyond conventional dietary recommendations, providing practical tips and tricks for implementing sustainable lifestyle changes. You will learn about managing your carbohydrate intake, exploring low potassium, low sodium, and low phosphorus recipes, and mitigating the risk of complications, all aimed at supporting your overall well-being.

To further assist you in your diabetes management journey, we offer a comprehensive 30-day meal plan. Organizing your meals, maintaining a healthy diet, and effectively managing your blood sugar levels become effortless with a well-structured selection of recipes. By customizing your approach based on your specific type of diabetes, you will have the tools to take proactive actions that suit your needs.

We have cracked the code on the ultimate diabetic feast!

Our aim is to empower you to make positive changes through a comprehensive understanding of diabetes exploring various diabetes types, adopting a diabetic-friendly diet, and providing a wealth of recipes.

In this cookbook,
we have whipped up a feast of diabetes-friendly recipes that will have you saying,
"Who knew healthy could taste this good?"

We want you to feel confident in making educated decisions about your lifestyle, nutrition and available recipes. This book sets the foundation for you to take charge of your diabetes and improve your overall well-being.

As we embark on this journey towards a healthier and more fulfilling life through cooking, let us start by laying the groundwork in Chapter 1. We will provide essential information about diabetes, its causes, and how it can affect our bodies. Understanding these basics will help us make better choices and care for ourselves as we move forward.

So, let us get started with Chapter 1 for an insightful journey.

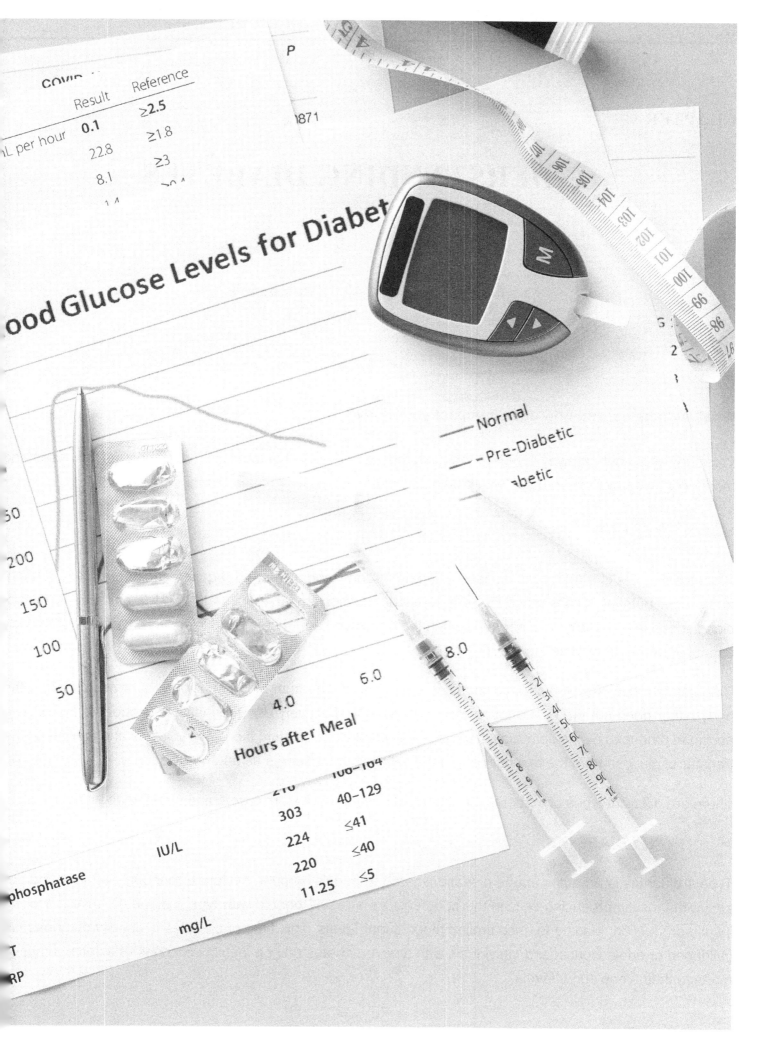

CHAPTER 1

UNDERSTANDING DIABETES

Diabetes is a great example whereby you can manage yourself by giving the patient the tools.

- Clayton M. Christensen!

What is diabetes, and how does it impact your body?

This chapter is your gateway to comprehending the ins and outs of diabetes. From symptoms to causes and monitoring, we have covered you with essential insights for effective diabetes management.

WHAT IS DIABETES?

Diabetes mellitus is a metabolic disease affecting millions worldwide and requires constant care, attention and proper nutrition. Diabetes could be a constant infection that influences the body's capacity to control blood sugar. Insulin resistance happens when the pancreas cannot create sufficient affront or when the body cannot appropriately utilize the affront it produces.

Diabetes is a complex and chronic condition characterized by high blood sugar levels. It occurs when the body either does not produce enough insulin or cannot effectively use the insulin it produces. Insulin is a hormone produced by the pancreas. It plays a crucial role in regulating blood sugar levels and facilitating the transfer of glucose from the bloodstream to the cells, where it serves as an energy source.

There are different types of diabetes, but the most common ones are type 1 and type 2 diabetes:

► *TYPE 1 DIABETES:*

Type 1 diabetes is an autoimmune disease where the body's immune system erroneously attacks and destroys the insulin-producing cells in the pancreas. As a result, people with type 1 diabetes have low or no insulin production, leading to uncontrolled blood sugar levels. This type of diabetes is usually diagnosed in childhood or adolescence, and individuals with type 1 diabetes rely on insulin injections or insulin pumps to manage their blood sugar levels.

▶ *TYPE 2 DIABETES:*

Type 2 diabetes is the most prevalent form of diabetes, accounting for about 90-95% of all cases. It usually develops later in life and is often associated with lifestyle factors, such as poor dietary choices, physical inactivity, and obesity. In type 2 diabetes, the body becomes insulin resistant, meaning that the cells do not respond properly to insulin's actions, or the pancreas doesn't produce enough insulin to meet the body's needs. As a result, blood sugar levels rise, leading to hyperglycemia. Initially, type 2 diabetes can often be managed through lifestyle changes, such as adopting a healthier diet, increasing physical activity, and losing weight. However, some individuals may require oral medications or insulin therapy to control their blood sugar effectively.

▶ *GESTATIONAL DIABETES:*

Another form of diabetes is gestational diabetes, which occurs during pregnancy. It affects about 2-10% of pregnant women and usually develops around the 24th to 28th week of pregnancy. Gestational diabetes can pose risks to both the mother and baby, so it is crucial to monitor and manage blood sugar levels during pregnancy closely. While gestational diabetes typically goes away after childbirth, women with a history of gestational diabetes have a higher risk of developing type 2 diabetes later in life.

SYMPTOMS OF DIABETES

The symptoms of diabetes can vary depending on the type and severity of the condition. Common symptoms include:

- ▶ Frequent urination (polyuria): High blood sugar levels can cause excess sugar to be eliminated through urine, leading to increased urination frequency.
- ▶ Excessive thirst (polydipsia): Frequent urination can result in dehydration, causing persistent thirst.
- ▶ Unexplained weight loss: Despite increased hunger and food intake, the body may not be able to use glucose for energy properly, leading to weight loss.
- ▶ Fatigue and weakness: Without sufficient glucose entering the cells, the body lacks energy, leading to fatigue and weakness.
- ▶ Blurred vision: High blood sugar levels can cause fluid buildup in the eye's lens, leading to blurred vision.
- ▶ Delayed wound healing: Diabetes can impair blood circulation and weaken the body's ability to heal wounds and fight infections.

It is important to note that some people with diabetes may not experience noticeable symptoms, especially in the early stages. Regular checkups and diabetes screenings are crucial for early detection and timely management of the condition.

CAUSES OF DIABETES

The causes of diabetes can vary depending on the type of diabetes:

- ▶ Type 1 Diabetes: Type 1 diabetes is believed to result from genetic predisposition and environmental triggers. In this type, the body's immune system mistakenly attacks and destroys the insulin-producing beta cells in the pancreas, leading to a lack of insulin production.

► Type 2 Diabetes: Type 2 diabetes is influenced by genetic factors and lifestyle choices. Factors such as a sedentary lifestyle, unhealthy diet, excess body weight, and family history of diabetes can increase the risk of developing type 2 diabetes.

► Gestational Diabetes: The exact cause of gestational diabetes is not entirely understood, but hormonal changes during pregnancy may lead to insulin resistance, resulting in elevated blood sugar levels.

DIAGNOSING AND MONITORING DIABETES

To diagnose diabetes, doctors can perform various tests, including fasting blood glucose, oral tolerance test, or glycosylated hemoglobin (A1C) tests. These tests help determine the glucose level in the blood and whether a person has diabetes. Diabetes monitoring involves regular blood sugar monitoring using a blood glucose meter or continuous blood glucose monitor (CGM). The following are some important aspects of proper diabetes care:

► *BLOOD GLUCOSE TESTING*

Regular blood glucose testing is the cornerstone of diabetes management. This includes using a glucometer to measure your blood sugar. The test should follow the doctor's instructions, which will vary depending on the type of diabetes and personal circumstances. Blood glucose monitoring allows people to understand how their bodies respond to different foods, physical activity, medications, and general management strategies.

► *A1C TESTING*

The A1C test gives the average blood sugar levels over the past two to three months. measures the rate of glycated hemoglobin. Doctors often do A1C testing as an indicator of long-term diabetes control. It helps evaluate the effectiveness of overall diabetes management and advises physicians to make necessary adjustments in treatment.

► *CONTINUOUS GLUCOSE MONITORING (CGM)*

This uses a small sensor placed under the skin to measure the glucose level in the liquid medium. CGM systems provide recommendations for diet, exercise, medications, and other factors related to diabetes.

Blood pressure self-monitoring helps to know the increased risk of hypertension in diabetics. Regular blood pressure monitoring at home with a sphygmomanometer is essential for diagnosing and controlling high blood pressure.

Furthermore, regular monitoring allows people to understand how their bodies respond to different foods, medications, and activities to make informed decisions about managing their blood sugar. By regularly monitoring blood sugar, A1C results, blood pressure, and other parameters, people with diabetes can take control of their health.

STAGES OF DIABETES

Diabetes can be divided into several stages according to the stage of diabetes and the development of the disease. These stages include prediabetes, type 2 diabetes, and high blood pressure. In diabetes mellitus, blood sugar levels are higher than normal but not high enough to be classified as type 2 diabetes.

➤ PREDIABETES

Prediabetes is characterized by blood sugar higher than normal but not high enough to be classified as diabetes. Prediabetes often indicates an increased risk of developing type 2 diabetes. Without intervention and proper management, many people with type 2 diabetes can develop complications. Lifestyle changes such as a healthy diet, increased physical activity, and weight control can help prevent or delay the onset of type 2 diabetes.

➤ TYPE 2 DIABETES

Type 2 diabetes is the most common type of diabetes, including most patients. It is often progressive and associated with lifestyle factors such as poor dietary choices, poor physical activity, and being overweight. In type 2 diabetes, the body becomes insulin resistant and cannot produce enough insulin to control blood sugar normally. This results in high blood sugar levels that require continued management with lifestyle changes, oral medications, and in some cases, insulin therapy.

➤ GESTATIONAL DIABETES

Gestational diabetes occurs during pregnancy and affects 2-10% of pregnant women. It must be carefully monitored and managed to ensure the health of the mother and child. Although gestational diabetes usually goes away after giving birth, women with gestational diabetes are at risk of developing type 2 diabetes later in life.

CHAPTER SUMMARY

Understanding the complexities of diabetes is the first step toward effectively managing this condition. By controlling diabetes in all stages, people can reduce the impact of the disease in daily life and maintain a good quality of life.

In the subsequent chapters, we will delve into the different types of diabetes and explore healthy meal plans and recipes to help you lead a vibrant and active life. *Stay tuned for more insightful information on diabetes management in the upcoming chapters. We will take charge of diabetes and embrace a healthier and happier life.*

CHAPTER 2

EXPLORING DIFFERENT FORMS OF DIABETES

Let food be thy medicine, and medicine be thy food.
- Hippocrates

Ready to unlock the puzzle of diabetes?

Diabetes is a chronic condition that impacts a substantial number of individuals worldwide, and it is crucial to recognize that not all cases of diabetes are identical. By delving into the distinct types of diabetes, we can better understand their unique characteristics, causes, approaches to management, and implications for overall well-being.

The purpose of this chapter is to offer a comprehensive overview of the most prevalent types of diabetes, including Type 1 diabetes, Type 2 diabetes, gestational diabetes, as well as other less common variants. Furthermore, it emphasizes the importance of individualized diabetes management and tailored treatment methods.

Unravel the diverse world of diabetes with this chapter!

TYPE 1 DIABETES

Type 1 diabetes, alternatively referred to as insulin-dependent diabetes or juvenile-onset diabetes, is an autoimmune condition where the immune system erroneously targets and eliminates the pancreatic cells responsible for producing insulin. Consequently, insulin is insufficient, a vital hormone that regulates sugar levels in the bloodstream.

CAUSES AND RISK FACTORS

The precise reasons behind Type 1 diabetes remain incompletely comprehended, and it is widely believed that genetic and environmental factors contribute significantly. Those with a familial predisposition to Type 1 diabetes are at a greater risk of developing the condition. Additionally, specific viral infections and exposure to environmental elements, such as dietary patterns during early childhood or a deficiency in vitamin D, may also play a role in the onset of Type 1 diabetes.

▶ SYMPTOMS AND DIAGNOSIS

Type 1 diabetes manifests suddenly, characterized by excessive thirst, frequent urination, unexplained weight loss, fatigue, and blurry vision. Diagnostic procedures involve blood tests to assess blood glucose levels and identify the presence of autoantibodies associated with the destruction of cells responsible for producing insulin.

▶ MANAGEMENT AND TREATMENT OPTIONS

Insulin therapy stands as the foremost approach for treating Type 1 diabetes. Insulin is administered through injections or an insulin pump to maintain optimal blood sugar levels. Alongside insulin therapy, individuals with Type 1 diabetes must regularly monitor their blood glucose levels, follow a balanced diet, engage in routine physical activity, and address other aspects of their overall health to avert complications.

▶ CHALLENGES AND COMPLICATIONS

Living with Type 1 diabetes can present various challenges, including constant monitoring of blood glucose levels, insulin injections, and a heightened risk of hypoglycemia and hyperglycemia. Long-term complications may include cardiovascular disease, kidney damage, nerve damage, and eye problems if blood sugar levels are poorly controlled over time.

It is time to explore the next type - Type 2 Diabetes. Read on!

TYPE 2 DIABETES

Type 2 diabetes, also known as non-insulin-dependent diabetes or adult-onset diabetes, is a metabolic disorder characterized by insulin resistance and impaired insulin secretion. In this form of diabetes, the body cannot effectively use insulin or produce enough to maintain normal blood sugar levels.

→ Causes and Risk Factors

Type 2 diabetes arises from a complex interplay of genetic and environmental factors. Key risk factors include obesity, lack of physical activity, an unhealthy diet, having a family history of diabetes, and increasing age. Ethnicity and certain medical conditions like polycystic ovary syndrome (PCOS) or prediabetes further enhance the likelihood of developing Type 2 diabetes.

▶ SYMPTOMS AND DIAGNOSIS

Symptoms of Type 2 diabetes typically exhibit a more gradual onset and tend to be less severe. Common indications encompass heightened thirst, frequent urination, fatigue, blurred vision, delayed wound healing, and recurrent infections. Diagnosis is commonly accomplished through blood tests that assess fasting blood glucose levels or employ an oral glucose tolerance test.

► MANAGEMENT AND TREATMENT OPTIONS

The treatment of Type 2 diabetes involves making changes to one's lifestyle, which includes adopting a nutritious diet, participating in regular physical activity, and potentially losing weight if needed. Depending on the situation, healthcare providers may also prescribe oral medications or insulin therapy to regulate blood sugar levels. It is essential to regularly monitor blood glucose, blood pressure, and cholesterol levels to ensure effective management of the condition.

► LIFESTYLE CHANGES AND PREVENTION

One of the critical aspects of managing Type 2 diabetes is making sustainable lifestyle changes. Options for managing Type 2 diabetes may involve adopting a balanced eating plan that prioritizes whole foods, portion management, and reducing the consumption of sugary and processed foods. Additionally, regular participation in physical activities like aerobic exercises and strength training can enhance insulin sensitivity. Preventive measures, such as maintaining a healthy weight, managing stress levels, and regular health checkups, can reduce the risk of developing Type 2 diabetes.

GESTATIONAL DIABETES

Gestational diabetes mellitus (GDM) is a transient type of diabetes that specifically emerges during pregnancy. It is distinguished by elevated blood sugar levels that either emerge or become apparent for the first-time during pregnancy.

CAUSES AND RISK FACTORS

The hormonal changes during pregnancy can affect insulin action, leading to gestational diabetes. Women who are overweight, have a family history of diabetes, had gestational diabetes in previous pregnancies, or belong to specific ethnic groups (such as South Asian, Hispanic, or African descent) are at a higher risk.

SYMPTOMS AND DIAGNOSIS

Gestational diabetes often does not present any noticeable symptoms. It is typically diagnosed through a glucose challenge test or an oral glucose tolerance test, which assesses how well the body processes sugar.

MANAGEMENT AND TREATMENT OPTIONS

To effectively handle gestational diabetes, it is crucial to regulate blood glucose levels within a specified range through dietary adjustments, consistent physical activity, and continuous monitoring of blood sugar levels. In certain situations, the administration of insulin injections may be required. Maintaining appropriate blood sugar levels during pregnancy is vital to avert complications for both the mother and the baby.

▶ *IMPLICATIONS FOR PREGNANCY AND LONG-TERM HEALTH*

If gestational diabetes is left untreated or inadequately managed, the likelihood of complications during pregnancy and delivery rises. These complications may include high blood pressure, preeclampsia, or the need for a cesarean section. Furthermore, there is an increased risk of developing Type 2 diabetes later in life for both the mother and the child. Therefore, women with gestational diabetes should undergo regular postpartum screening and adopt healthy lifestyle habits to reduce their future risk.

Till now, we have covered Type 1 and Type 2 diabetes. There are many other less common types of Diabetes; let us look at them!

OTHER LESS COMMON TYPES OF DIABETES

While Type 1 and Type 2 diabetes are the most well-known forms, several other less common types warrant attention and understanding.

▶ *MODY (MATURITY-ONSET DIABETES OF THE YOUNG)*

Maturity-Onset Diabetes of the Young (MODY) is a rare type of diabetes triggered by a genetic mutation that impacts insulin production. Typically occurring before the age of twenty-five, MODY is frequently misidentified as either Type 1 or Type 2 diabetes.

▶ *LADA (LATENT AUTOIMMUNE DIABETES OF ADULTHOOD)*

LADA (Latent Autoimmune Diabetes in Adults) is a gradually developing autoimmune form of diabetes exhibiting traits found in Type 1 and Type 2 diabetes. It commonly manifests in adulthood and is initially misdiagnosed as Type 2 diabetes due to its slow onset.

▶ *SECONDARY DIABETES*

An underlying medical condition or certain medications cause secondary diabetes. For example, pancreatic diseases, hormonal disorders, or the use of corticosteroids can lead to secondary diabetes.

▶ *OTHER RARE FORMS*

There are various other rare forms of diabetes, such as neonatal diabetes, mitochondrial diabetes, and Wolfram syndrome. These forms are usually diagnosed in infancy or childhood and require specialized care.

UNIQUE CHARACTERISTICS AND MANAGEMENT APPROACHES

Each less common type of diabetes has unique characteristics, diagnostic criteria, and management approaches. Understanding these specific forms of diabetes is crucial for accurate diagnosis and effective management.

PERSONALIZED DIABETES MANAGEMENT

Personalized diabetes management recognizes that everyone's diabetes experience is unique. Age, lifestyle, medical history, and specific diabetes type should be considered when developing a management plan. Tailored approaches consider individual needs, preferences, and goals, leading to more effective and satisfactory outcomes.

BENEFITS OF UNDERSTANDING SPECIFIC DIABETES TYPE

Understanding the specific type of diabetes, a person has is essential for appropriate management. Each type has distinct underlying causes, treatment options, and potential complications. Healthcare providers can make informed decisions regarding medication choices, lifestyle recommendations, and monitoring protocols by accurately identifying the type.

TARGETED TREATMENT STRATEGIES

Based on the type of diabetes, treatment strategies can be tailored to address specific needs. For example, individuals with Type 1 diabetes require lifelong insulin therapy, while those with Type 2 diabetes may benefit from oral medications, injectable medications, or a combination of both. Gestational diabetes may be managed through lifestyle modifications and, if necessary, insulin therapy during pregnancy. Less common types of diabetes often require specialized treatment and close monitoring.

Personalized diabetes management also involves regularly monitoring blood sugar levels, HbA1c levels, lipid profiles, and other relevant markers to assess the effectiveness of treatment and adjust the management plan accordingly. Additionally, it includes ongoing education and support to empower individuals with diabetes to make informed decisions and actively participate in their self-care.

CHAPTER SUMMARY

Understanding the different forms of diabetes is crucial for healthcare professionals, individuals with diabetes, and their loved ones. Each type of diabetes has unique characteristics, risk factors, and management approaches. By recognizing these differences, healthcare providers can deliver more targeted and effective care, diabetes can make informed decisions about their lifestyle, treatment options, and self-management.

Want to master the art of mindful eating?

Let Chapter 3 guide you toward a healthier and more balanced lifestyle.

Trying to manage diabetes is hard!

BECAUSE IF YOU DON'T...
There are consequences you'll have to deal with later in life.

CHAPTER 3

DIABETIC DIET

*Cooking has never been so sweet - just like our
sugar-free desserts!!*

Living with diabetes requires careful attention to diet and nutrition. A well-planned and balanced diet is essential for effectively managing diabetes and maintaining overall health. This chapter will explore the significance of a diabetic diet and provide guidelines and recommendations for creating a meal plan that supports stable blood sugar levels and promotes well-being. By making informed and healthy food choices, you can take control of your health and manage diabetes with confidence.

RECOMMENDED FOODS IN DIABETIC DIET

When managing diabetes, making the right food choices is crucial. Here, we will discuss a comprehensive list of foods that are considered suitable for a diabetic diet:

Low-glycemic index foods: These foods have a minimal impact on blood sugar levels. Examples include non-starchy vegetables, legumes, whole grains, and most fruits.

High-fiber options: Foods rich in dietary fibre help regulate blood sugar levels and promote digestive health. Include whole grains, vegetables, fruits, and legumes in your diet.

Lean protein sources: Opt for lean proteins such as skinless poultry, fish, tofu, beans, and lentils. These proteins provide essential nutrients without adding excess fat or cholesterol.

Nutrient-rich fruits and vegetables: Incorporate a variety of colorful fruits and vegetables into your meals. They provide essential vitamins, minerals, and antioxidants, promoting overall health.

To incorporate these recommended foods into your daily meal plans, consider the following practical tips:

Fill half of your plate with non-starchy vegetables.
Choose whole grains over refined grains.
Include a moderate portion of lean protein in each meal.
Enjoy fresh fruits as snacks or dessert options.

Remember, sustainable changes in your diet are essential to long-term diabetes management. Gradually incorporate these foods into your routine and make them a part of your healthy lifestyle.

BENEFITS OF A DIABETIC DIET

Following a diabetic diet offers several benefits for individuals with diabetes:

Regulating blood sugar levels: By choosing foods that have a minimal impact on blood sugar, you can better manage your glucose levels and prevent sudden spikes or drops.

- ▶ Maintaining a healthy weight: A diabetic diet focuses on portion control and nutrient-dense foods, which can aid in weight management. Sustaining an optimal weight is crucial for effectively managing diabetes and minimizing the chances of experiencing complications.
- ▶ Reducing the risk of complications: By following a diabetic diet, you can lower the risk of complications associated with diabetes, such as heart disease, stroke, and kidney problems.

Numerous studies have demonstrated the positive effects of a well-planned diabetic diet on glucose control and overall health. You can significantly improve your well-being by incorporating these dietary changes.

CREATING A DIABETIC-FRIENDLY MEAL PLAN

Our secret ingredient? A sprinkle of love and a dash of diabetic wisdom!

To create a diabetic-friendly meal plan, consider the following factors:

- ▶ Portion control and mindful eating habits: Be mindful of the amount of food you consume and be attuned to your body's signals of hunger and satisfaction. Steers clear of excessive eating and adopts a mindful approach to eating by relishing each mouthful and taking your time.
- ▶ Designing a well-balanced meal plan: Aim to include a variety of food groups in each meal, including carbohydrates, proteins, and fats. Distribute your daily calorie intake evenly throughout the day.
- ▶ Carbohydrate sources: Keep a close watch on the amount of carbohydrates you consume and choose complex carbohydrates like whole grains, legumes, and vegetables. These carbohydrates are metabolized more gradually and have a minor effect on blood sugar levels.
- ▶ Protein and fat sources: Choose lean proteins like poultry, fish, and tofu, and incorporate healthy fats such as avocados, nuts, and olive oil. These foods provide essential nutrients while keeping saturated fats and cholesterol in check.
- ▶ Meal planning for different times: Plan your breakfast, lunch, dinner, and snacks. Include a balance of carbohydrates, proteins, and fats in each meal, and consider spacing your meals throughout the day to maintain stable blood sugar levels.
- ▶ Individual preferences and cultural considerations: Customize your meal plan according to your dietary preferences and cultural background. Diabetes management can be tailored to suit different culinary traditions.

OTHER CONSIDERATIONS FOR DIABETIC DIET

In addition to a well-planned meal plan, there are other essential considerations for managing diabetes e ectively:

Monitoring carbohydrate intake and glycemic load: Keep track of the carbohydrates you consume and learn about different foods' glycemic index and glycemic load. This knowledge will help you make informed decisions about your diet.

The role of carbohydrates in blood sugar management: Understand the impact of carbohydrates on blood sugar levels and learn to balance your carbohydrate intake with insulin or other medications. Consult with your healthcare team for personalized guidance.

The importance of regular physical activity: Alongside a diabetic diet, engage in regular physical activity to improve insulin sensitivity, maintain a healthy weight, and enhance overall well-being. Aim for a combination of aerobic exercises and strength training.

Managing stress and its impact on blood sugar levels: Stress can affect blood sugar control. Explore stress management techniques such as meditation, deep breathing exercises, and engaging in hobbies or activities that bring you joy.

Consulting a healthcare professional or registered dietitian: Seek guidance from healthcare professionals or registered dietitians specializing in diabetes management. They can provide personalized advice tailored to your needs and help you navigate challenges.

CHAPTER SUMMARY

In a nutshell, the chapter on the diabetic diet highlights the significance of a well-planned and balanced diet in managing diabetes effectively. By incorporating recommended foods, practicing portion control, and making mindful food choices, you can regulate blood sugar levels, maintain a healthy weight, and reduce the risk of complications associated with diabetes.

Managing diabetes is a lifelong journey, and taking control of your diet can positively impact your health and well-being.

So why wait?

Start exploring these recipes today and experience the delightful and wholesome journey of a diabetic-friend-
diet.

CHAPTER 4

WHAT TO EXPECT IN THIS COOKBOOK?

Ever tried to high-five a chef?

You will after tasting our diabetic delights!

Welcome to a cookbook that's more than just recipes!

In this chapter, we will explore the key takeaways you can expect to find throughout the book, setting the stage for your journey towards healthier and more enjoyable eating.

➤ PRACTICAL GUIDANCE FOR MANAGING DIABETIC DIET

To effectively manage your diabetic diet, it is essential to have practical guidance that helps you understand and implement dietary recommendations. This book aims to provide just that. We will offer clear explanations of the principles behind a diabetic-friendly diet, step-by-step instructions for making dietary changes, and valuable tips to ensure you can easily incorporate these changes into your daily life. We aim to empower you with the knowledge and tools necessary to navigate your diabetic diet successfully.

➤ NUTRITIOUS AND DELICIOUS RECIPES FOR INDIVIDUALS WITH DIABETES

Eating well with diabetes does not mean sacrificing flavor and enjoyment. This cookbook offers diverse, nutritious, and delicious recipes for individuals managing diabetes. We understand that eating should be a pleasurable experience, and we have carefully crafted recipes that are not only diabetes-friendly but also bursting with flavor. From savory main courses to delectable desserts, you can discover a world of culinary delights that align with your dietary requirements.

➤ MEAL PLANNING ASSISTANCE FOR DIABETIC-FRIENDLY MEALS

Meal planning is crucial in maintaining stable blood sugar levels and overall health. To simplify this process, our cookbook provides valuable assistance with meal planning. We offer sample meal plans that take the guesswork out of creating balanced and diabetic-friendly meals. These plans will help you understand portion sizes, appropriate combinations of nutrients, and the timing of your meals. Additionally, we provide guidelines and practical tips to help you create well-rounded meal plans tailored to your personal preferences and dietary needs. Each plan includes breakfast, lunch, dinner, and snack options, providing inspiration and guidance for your meal planning.

Let us look at some examples:

Breakfast:

- ▶ Option 1: Veggie omelet with spinach, bell peppers, and feta cheese, served with whole-grain toast.
- ▶ Option 2: Overnight oats with mixed berries and chopped nuts sprinkled.
- ▶ Option 3: Greek yogurt topped with sliced bananas, almonds, and a drizzle of honey.

Lunch:

- ▶ Option 1: Grilled chicken salad with mixed greens, cherry tomatoes, cucumber, and a light vinaigrette dressing.
- ▶ Option 2: Quinoa and roasted vegetable bowl with chickpeas and a lemon tahini dressing.
- ▶ Option 3: Whole grain wrap filled with turkey, avocado, lettuce, and tomato, served with carrot sticks.

Dinner:

- ▶ Option 1: Baked salmon with roasted asparagus and quinoa pilaf.
- ▶ Option 2: Stir-fried tofu and vegetables with brown rice.
- ▶ Option 3: Grilled chicken breast with steamed broccoli and sweet potato mash.

Snacks:

- ▶ Option 1: Apple slices with almond butter.
- ▶ Option 2: Greek yogurt with a sprinkle of granola.
- ▶ Option 3: Raw vegetables with hummus.

▶   *EDUCATION ON DIABETES MANAGEMENT*

Beyond providing a collection of recipes, this cookbook is committed to educating you about diabetes management. Understanding the basics of diabetes is essential for making informed choices about your diet and lifestyle. We will delve into the different types of diabetes, how it affects your body, and the importance of blood sugar control. By gaining a deeper understanding of diabetes management, you will be equipped with the knowledge to make proactive health decisions. Here are some guidelines and tips to help you with your meal planning:

- ▶ Portion control: Use measuring cups, food scales, or visual cues to ensure appropriate portion sizes of carbohydrates, proteins, and fats.
- ▶ Meal timing: Spread your meals and snacks evenly throughout the day to maintain stable blood sugar levels. Aim for three main meals and 2-3 snacks.
- ▶ Carbohydrate management: Choose complex carbohydrates high in fibre and have a lower glycemic index. Include a variety of vegetables, whole grains, and legumes in your meals.
- ▶ Protein choices: Opt for lean protein sources such as poultry, fish, tofu, and legumes. Avoid fried or processed meats.
- ▶ Healthy fats: Incorporate sources of healthy fats, such as avocados, nuts, seeds, and olive oil, in moderation.
- ▶ Hydration: Stay hydrated by drinking plenty of water throughout the day. Limit sugary beverages and opt for water, herbal tea, or unsweetened options.

▶   *EMPOWERMENT AND CONFIDENCE IN DIABETES MANAGEMENT*

Our goal is to empower you to take control of your health and develop sustainable hab s for long-term diabetes management. By providing practical guidance, nutritious reci-es, meal planning assistance, and education on diabetes management, this cookbook aims o instill confidence in your ability to manage your diabetic diet effectively. We want you to feel mpowered to make informed choices, overcome challenges, and embrace a healthier festyle. With this newfound confidence, you can navigate the world of diabetes management with ease and mbark on a journey of improved well-being.

CHAPTER SUMMARY

We have explored what you can expect in this comprehensive cookbook designed to upport individuals managing their diabetic diet. From practical guidance and delicious recipes o meal planning assistance, education on diabetes management, and the empowerment to take ontrol of your health, this cookbook is a valuable resource on your path toward a healthier and more fulfilling fe.

Our cookbook does not count calories!

It counts as smiles on your satisfied faces!

Say goodbye to bland and hello to the joy of deliciously wholesome meals.

****

Ready to dive into a world of delicious diabetic recipes?

Turn the page and let us start cooking in Chapter 5!

CHAPTER 5

BREAKFAST

1. Banana Pancakes

2. Asparagus Frittata

3. Cauliflower Scramble

4. Stuffed Tomatoes

5. Mushroom Omelette

6. Blueberry Pancakes

7. Cheesy Scrambled Eggs

8. Almond Berry Oatmeal

9. Pumpkin Spice Muffins

10. Seedy Muesli

11. Healthy Granola

12. Multigrain Avocado Toast

1. BANANA PANCAKES

Servings: 4   Duration: 20 minutes

INGREDIENTS	INSTRUCTIONS
• 2 ripe bananas • 2 large eggs • 1/2 cup almond flour • 1/2 tsp baking powder • 1/2 tsp ground cinnamon • 1/4 tsp salt • 1/4 cup unsweetened almond milk • 1 tbsp coconut oil (for cooking) • Sugar-free pancake syrup (optional for serving)	1. Mash bananas in a large bowl using a masher. Add eggs and mix them well. 2. Combine almond flour, baking powder, cinnamon, and salt in another bowl. 3. Gradually add the dry mixture to the banana mixture. 4. Pour in almond milk, stir, and mix until smooth. 5. Place a heavy skillet over medium-low heat, add coconut oil. 6. Pour ¼ cup batter onto skillet, cook until bubbles form, and the edges start to look set, approx. 2-3 minutes. 7. Flip pancakes using a spatula and cook until golden brown. 8. Repeat with the remaining batter. 9. Serve warm with sugar-free syrup.

NUTRIENTS (PER SERVINGS)

Carbs: 18g | Protein: 6g | Fat: 10g | Fiber: 4g | Sugar: 5g | Sodium: 260mg

2. ASPARAGUS FRITTATA

Servings: 4   Duration: 30 minutes

INGREDIENTS	INSTRUCTIONS
• 6 large eggs • 1 bunch(450g) of asparagus, trimmed and cut into pieces. • 1 small onion finely chopped. • 2 cloves of garlic, minced. • 1 tbsp olive oil • Salt and pepper to taste	1. Preheat oven to 375°F (190°C). 2. Sauté onion and garlic in olive oil until translucent. 3. Add asparagus and cook until tender. 4. Beat eggs in a bowl and pour over the asparagus mixture. 5. Cook the frittata on the stovetop for 2 to 3 minutes until the edges are set. 6. Transfer skillet to oven and bake for 15 minutes until lightly golden from top and set. 7. Sprinkle-grated Parmesan cheese on top (optional) to add flavor. 8. Allow it to cool slightly. Cut the frittata into slices and serve warm.

NUTRIENTS (PER SERVINGS)

Carbs: 5g | Protein: 12g | Fat: 13g | Fiber: 2g | Sugar: 2g | Sodium: 240mg

. CAULIFLOWER SCRAMBLE

Servings: 2   Duration: 25 minutes

INGREDIENTS	INSTRUCTIONS
<ul><li>2 cups cauliflower florets</li><li>4 large eggs</li><li>1 small onion finely chopped.</li><li>1 medium bell pepper, diced.</li><li>2 cloves garlic, minced.</li><li>2 tbsp olive oil</li><li>1/4 tsp turmeric powder</li><li>1/4 tsp cumin powder</li><li>Salt and pepper to taste</li></ul>	1. Pulse cauliflower florets in a food processor until rice-like. 2. In a heavy skillet, add onions, bell peppers, and garlic. Sauté the mixture until the onions and bell peppers become tender, usually taking about 3 to 4 minutes. 3. Now add cauliflower rice, turmeric, and cumin. 4. Cook for about 6-8 minutes. 5. Whisk eggs separately. 6. Push cauliflower to one side, pour eggs in the empty space, and let them set. 7. Scramble eggs into cauliflower and cook for 2-3 minutes additionally. 8. Season with salt and pepper. Serve hot.

NUTRIENTS (PER SERVINGS)

Fat: 13g | Saturated Fat: 2.8g | Cholesterol: 372mg | Sodium: 137mg | Carbs: 10g | Fiber: 3g | Sugars: 4g | Protein: 10g

. STUFFED TOMATOES

Servings: 4   Duration: 35 minutes

INGREDIENTS	INSTRUCTIONS
<ul><li>4 large tomatoes</li><li>4 large eggs</li><li>1/4 cup chopped spinach.</li><li>1/4 cup diced bell pepper.</li><li>1/4 cup diced onion.</li><li>2 cloves garlic, minced.</li><li>1 tbsp olive oil</li><li>Salt and pepper, to taste.</li><li>Fresh parsley or basil for garnish (optional)</li></ul>	1. Preheat the oven to 375°F (190°C). 2. Cut the tops of the tomatoes and scoop out the pulp and seeds. 3. Heat the oil, sauté garlic, onion, and bell pepper in a skillet until tender. Add chopped spinach and cook until wilted. Remove from heat. 4. Place tomato shells in a baking dish. Fill each tomato shell with the cooked vegetable mixture. 5. Crack one egg into each tomato shell. Sprinkle salt and pepper over each egg. 6. Bake in preheated oven for 15-20 minutes until the eggs fit in. Let the stuffed tomatoes cool slightly. 7. Garnish with fresh parsley or basil, if desired. Serve and enjoy!

NUTRIENTS (PER SERVINGS)

Saturated Fat: 2g | Cholesterol: 186mg | Sodium: 82mg | Carbs: 8g | Fiber: 2g | Sugars: 4g | Protein: 8g

5. MUSHROOM OMELETTE

Servings: 1   Duration: 15 minutes

INGREDIENTS	INSTRUCTIONS
• 2 large eggs • 1/2 cup sliced mushrooms. • 1/4 cup diced onion. • 1 clove garlic, minced. • 1 tbsp olive oil • Salt and pepper, to taste. • Fresh herbs (optional)	1. Heat olive oil in a skillet over medium heat. 2. Sauté onion and garlic until translucent. 3. Add mushrooms and cook for 2-3 minutes until tender. 4. In a separate bowl, whisk the eggs well and season with salt and pepper. 5. Pour eggs into the skillet and cook until almost set. 6. Add mushroom mixture onto one side of the omelet. Fold the other half over the filling. 7. Cook for another minute to heat the filling and fully cook the omelet. 8. Slide onto a plate and garnish with fresh herbs. Serve hot.

NUTRIENTS (PER SERVINGS)

Cholesterol: 372mg | Sodium: 175mg | Carbs: 5g | Fiber: 1g | Sugars: 2g | Protein: 12g

6. BLUEBERRY PANCAKES

Servings: 4   Duration: 25 minutes

INGREDIENTS	INSTRUCTIONS
• 1 cup whole wheat flour • 1 tbsp baking powder • 1/4 tsp salt • 2 tbsp sugar substitute • 1 cup unsweetened almond milk • 2 tbsp unsweetened apple-sauce • 1 tsp vanilla extract • 1 cup fresh blueberries • Cooking spray	1. Add flour, baking powder, salt, and sugar substitute in a mixing bowl. 2. Now take a separate bowl, and whisk almond milk, applesauce, and vanilla extract until smooth. 3. Gradually pour the wet ingredients into the dry ingredients and stir gently. 4. Gently fold in the blueberries. 5. Preheat a non-stick skillet and lightly coat with cooking spray. 6. Use a 1/4 cup measuring cup to pour pancake batter onto the skillet. 7. Cook until bubbles form on the surface, then flip and cook for 1-2 minutes. 8. Repeat with the remaining batter. 9. Drizzle with honey (optional) with remaining blueberries on top.

NUTRIENTS (PER SERVINGS)

Cholesterol: 0mg | Sodium: 385mg | Carbs: 38g | Dietary Fiber: 6g | Sugars: 5g | Protein: 5g

7. CHEESY SCRAMBLED EGGS

Servings: 2   Duration: 10 minutes

INGREDIENTS	INSTRUCTIONS
<ul><li>4 large eggs</li><li>1/4 cup low-fat milk</li><li>1/4 tsp. salt</li><li>1/4 tsp. black pepper</li><li>1 tbsp. unsalted butter</li><li>1/4 cup shredded low-fat cheddar cheese.</li><li>2 tbsp. chopped fresh chives (optional)</li></ul>	1. Add low-fat milk, salt, whisked eggs, and black pepper in a medium-sized bowl. 2. In a non-stick skillet over medium heat Melt unsalted butter. 3. Pour the egg mixture into the skillet and set it around the edges. 4. Gently stir the eggs, pushing them from the edges to the center. 5. Sprinkle shredded low-fat cheddar cheese over the eggs and continue stirring until melted and cooked to desired consistency. 6. Remove from heat and let residual heat finish cooking the eggs. 7. Sprinkle chopped fresh chives on top (optional). Serve hot with whole-grain toast or fresh vegetables.

NUTRIENTS (PER SERVINGS)

Carbs: 2g | Protein: 16g | Fat: 15g | Fiber: 0g | Cholesterol: 385mg | Sodium: 400mg | Potassium: 210mg

8. ALMOND BERRY OATMEAL

Servings: 2   Duration: 15 minutes

INGREDIENTS	INSTRUCTIONS
<ul><li>2 cups water</li><li>1/4 tsp. salt</li><li>1/2 tsp. cinnamon</li><li>1/4 cup unsweetened almond milk</li><li>1/4 tsp. vanilla extract</li><li>1 tbsp. natural almond butter</li><li>1 cup mixed berries</li><li>2 tbsp. sliced almonds.</li><li>1 tsp. honey or sugar substitute (optional)</li></ul>	1. Place a medium-sized saucepan over low-medium heat, and add rolled oats, salt, and water together. Cook for 5-10 minutes until softened or bring it to a boil. 2. Now stir in cinnamon, almond milk, and vanilla extract. Keep cooking for another 2-3 minutes; let all the flavors meld together. If 3. Now remove the saucepan from heat and add almond butter, stirring well. 4. Transfer the oatmeal to serving bowls. Top with mixed berries and sliced almonds. 5. Drizzle with honey (if desired) or sugar substitute.

NUTRIENTS (PER SERVINGS)

Carbs: 38g | Protein: 9g | Fat: 11g | Fiber: 8g | Sugar: 8g | Sodium: 230mg

. PUMPKIN SPICE MUFFINS

ervings: 12   Duration: 30-35 minutes

INGREDIENTS

- 1 ½ cups almond flour
- ½ cup coconut flour
- 2 tsp baking powder
- 1 tsp cinnamon
- ½ tsp nutmeg
- ¼ tsp cloves
- ¼ tsp salt, 3 eggs
- ½ cup unsweetened pumpkin
- ½ cup unsweetened applesauce
- ¼ cup melted coconut oil
- ¼ cup unsweetened almond milk
- 1 tsp vanilla extract
- 10-12 drops liquid stevia (or preferred sweetener)
- Optional: Chopped walnuts or pecans

INSTRUCTIONS

1. Preheat the oven to 350°F (175°C).
2. Line a muffin tin with paper liners.
3. Put the almond flour, coconut flour, baking powder, cinnamon, nutmeg, cloves, and salt in a medium bowl. Mix and set aside.
4. Add melted coconut oil in another medium bowl, mix pumpkin, applesauce, eggs, almond milk, vanilla extract, and liquid stevia.
5. Add the wet mixture to the dry ingredients gradually and stir until well mixed.
6. Now divide the batter evenly among the muffin cups and fill each cup about 3/4 full.
7. Sprinkle chopped walnuts on the top of each muffin.
8. Bake for 20-25 minutes or until a toothpick comes out clean after being inserted in muffins.
9. Let the muffins cool in a tin for a while, serve with a latte and enjoy!

NUTRIENTS (PER SERVINGS)

Cholesterol: 47mg | Sodium: 118mg | Total Carbs: 7g | Dietary Fiber: 3g | Sugars: 1g | Protein: 5g

0. SEEDY MUESLI

ervings: 4   Duration: 15 minutes

INGREDIENTS

- 1 cup rolled oats.
- 1/4 cup unsalted sunflower seeds
- 1/4 cup unsalted pumpkin seeds
- 1/4 cup flaxseeds
- 1/4 cup chia seeds
- 1/4 cup unsweetened shredded coconut
- 1/4 cup chopped almonds.
- 1/4 cup chopped walnuts.
  1/4 cup dried cranberries 1 teaspoon ground cinnamon

INSTRUCTIONS

1. Add the rolled oats, sunflower seeds, pumpkin seeds, flaxseeds, chia seeds, ground cinnamon, almonds, walnuts, dried cranberries, and shredded coconut in a large mixing bowl.
2. Mix everything together until they are well combined. Ensure that the cinnamon is evenly distributed throughout the mixture.
3. You can store the seedy muesli in an airtight container or jar. It can be saved at room temperature for up to two weeks.

Carbs: 25g | Protein: 8g | Fiber: 7g | Healthy Fats: 14g | Sugar: 4g | Sodium: 5mg

11. HEALTHY GRANOLA

Servings: 8   Duration: 20-30 minutes

INGREDIENTS	INSTRUCTIONS
<ul><li>2 cups rolled oats.</li><li>1 cup chopped unsalted almonds.</li><li>1/2 cup chopped unsalted walnuts.</li><li>1/2 cup unsalted pumpkin seeds</li><li>1/4 cup flaxseeds</li><li>1/4 cup chia seeds</li><li>1/2 tsp. ground cinnamon</li><li>1/4 tsp. salt</li><li>1/4 cup melted coconut oil.</li><li>1/4 cup sugar-free maple syrup or sugar substitute</li><li>1 tsp. vanilla extract</li><li>1 cup unsweetened dried cranberries or blueberries</li></ul>	1. Preheat the oven to 325°F (165°C), and line a baking sheet with parchment paper. 2. Combine almonds, walnuts, pumpkin seeds, flaxseeds, chia seeds, cinnamon, and salt together in a large bowl. 3. Whisk coconut oil, maple syrup (or sugar substitute), and vanilla extract in another separate bowl. 4. Pour the liquid mixture over the dry ingredients and stir everything evenly. 5. Now spread the mixture on the baking sheet and press it down gently. Bake for 25-30 minutes, stirring occasionally, until golden brown. 6. Let it cool completely on the baking sheet. 7. Optional: Add dried cranberries or blueberries. 8. Store in an airtight container.

NUTRIENTS (PER SERVINGS)

Carbs: 23g | Fiber: 5g | Sugar: 4g | Protein: 8g

12. MULTIGRAIN AVOCADO TOAST

Servings: 2   Duration: 15 minutes

INGREDIENTS	INSTRUCTIONS
<ul><li>2 slices multigrain bread</li><li>1 ripe avocado</li><li>1 tbsp. lemon juice</li><li>1/2 tsp. garlic powder</li><li>1/4 tsp. sea salt</li><li>Pinch of black pepper</li><li>1 tsp. extra-virgin olive oil</li><li>Optional toppings: cherry tomatoes, sprouts, crushed red pepper flakes</li></ul>	1. Toast multigrain bread slices until they are crispy and golden brown. 2. Mash avocado with lemon juice, garlic powder, salt, and pepper in a large bowl. 3. Spread mashed avocado on toasted bread slices evenly. 4. Drizzle 1 tsp. of extra-virgin olive oil over avocado spread on each slice. 5. Add optional toppings like cherry tomatoes, sprouts, and crushed red pepper flakes, if desired. 6. Serve the multigrain avocado toast immediately while the bread is still warm, and the avocado is fresh. 7. Serve and enjoy!

NUTRIENTS (PER SERVINGS)

Carbs: 22g | Fiber: 9g | Protein: 6g | Sodium: 220mg

CHAPTER 6

SOUPS & STEWS

1. Mexican Tortilla Soup

2. Turkey & Rice Soup

3. Tasty Tomato Soup

4. Creamy Mushroom Soup

5. Minestrone with Parmigiano Reggiano

6. Pumpkin Soup

7. White Bean Soup

8. Creamy Broccoli Soup

9. Butternut Squash Soup

10. Lentil Soup

. MEXICAN TORTILLA SOUP

Servings: 4   Duration: 25 minutes

INGREDIENTS

- 1 tb sp olive oil
- 2 cloves garlic, minced.
- 1 jalapeño pepper, diced.
- 1 red bell pepper, diced.
- 4 cups low-sodium chicken or vegetable broth
- 1 zucchini, diced.
- 1 can (14.5 oz) non-sugar-added diced tomatoes.
- 1 tsp cumin
- 1 small onion, diced.
- 1 cup corn kernels
- 1 tsp chili powder
- 1 cup cooked shredded chicken breast.
- 1 tsp dried oregano
- Salt and pepper to taste
- Juice of 1 lime
- Baked tortilla chips (crushed, optional)
- Avocado slices (optional)

INSTRUCTIONS

1. In a heavy large skillet, heat the olive oil. Add onions, garlic, jalapeño, and red bell pepper, and sauté until tender.
2. Add the zucchini, diced tomatoes, broth, cumin, chili powder, oregano, salt, and pepper. Bring to a boil, then let it cook slowly for 15 minutes. Stir occasionally.
3. Add chicken shreds and corn, and simmer for 5 minutes more.
4. Remove the soup from the heat and stir in the lime juice. If necessary, change the flavor.
5. Pour it into bowls. Add parsley as a garnish. You can add crushed tortilla chips and pieces of avocado if you want.
6. Serve warmly. Enjoy!

NUTRIENTS (PER SERVINGS)

Carbs: 28g | Protein: 20g | Fat: 6g | Fiber: 6g | Sugar: 8g | Sodium: 200mg

. TURKEY & RICE SOUP

Servings: 4   Duration: 40 minutes

INGREDIENTS

- 1 onion, diced.
- 3 cloves of garlic, minced.
- 1 tbsp of olive oil
- 4 cups of low-sodium turkey or chicken broth
- 1 cup of water
- 1 cup of cooked brown rice
- 2 cups of cooked turkey meat shredded or chopped.
- 2 carrots peeled and diced.
- 2 stalks of celery, diced.
- 1 tsp of dried thyme
- Salt and pepper to taste

INSTRUCTIONS

1. Heat the olive oil in a large pot over medium heat. Add the onions and garlic and sauté until soft.
2. Add the turkey or chicken broth and water to the pot and bring to a simmer.
3. Add the cooked brown rice, turkey meat, diced carrots, diced celery, and dried thyme to the pot.
4. Simmer the soup for about 20 minutes or until the vegetables are tender.
5. Season the soup with salt and pepper to taste.

NUTRIENTS (PER SERVINGS)

Cholesterol: 45mg | Sodium: 240mg | carbs: 19g | Sugar: 2g | Protein: 17g

3. TASTY TOMATO SOUP

Servings: 4   Duration: 30 minutes

INGREDIENTS	INSTRUCTIONS
• 2 tbsp olive oil • 1 onion, chopped. • 2 cloves garlic, minced. • 4 cups low-sodium vegetable broth • 4 large tomatoes, chopped. • 1 tsp dried basil • 1/2 tsp dried oregano • 1/2 tsp salt • 1/4 tsp black pepper • 1/2 cup heavy cream (optional)	1. Heat the olive oil in a big pot over medium-high heat. Add the onion and garlic and cook them together until the onion turns clear. 2. Put the chopped tomatoes, veggie broth, basil, oregano, salt, and pepper in the pot. Bring to a boil, then turn down the heat and let it simmer for 10 to 15 minutes or until the tomatoes are soft and cooked. 3. Turn off the stove and set the saucepan aside to cool for a while. 4. Use a hand-held mixer to make the soup smooth. 5. Add heavy cream, if using, and mix well. Simmer the soup for 2–3 minutes more. 6. Add more salt and pepper if needed.

NUTRIENTS (PER SERVINGS)

Cholesterol: 0mg | Sodium: 380mg | Carbs: 13g | Dietary fiber: 2g | Sugar: 7g | Protein: 2g

4. CREAMY MUSHROOM SOUP

Servings: 5   Duration: 25 minutes

INGREDIENTS	INSTRUCTIONS
• 2 tbsp reduced-calorie, trans-fat-free margarine. • 1/4 tsp garlic salt • 2 cans (14 ounces each) of fat-free beef broth • 1 package (8 ounces) crimini mushrooms, sliced. • 1/2 medium onion thinly sliced. • 1 can (6 ounces) tomato paste • 1/4 tsp coarse ground black pepper • 1 tbsp Worcestershire sauce • 1/4 tsp dried basil	1. Heat margarine in a large pan until it melts. 2. Add the mushrooms and onions and cook over medium heat, turning often, until the onions are clear, which should take about 5 minutes. 3. Mix the basil, pepper, garlic salt, and beef broth together and bring to a boil. 4. Then, lower the heat to medium and stir in tomato paste and Worcestershire sauce. Let the mixture warm up completely. Serve hot!

NUTRIENTS (PER SERVINGS)

Carbs: 11g | Protein: 7g | Fat: 2g | Sodium: 370g | Fiber: 2g

5. MINESTRONE WITH PARMIGIANO REGGIANO

Servings: 6   Duration: 25 minutes

INGREDIENTS

- 1 tbsp oil
- 2 cloves garlic, crushed.
- quarter Savoy cabbage, chopped.
- 1 large onion, chopped.
- 4 tbsp fresh parsley, chopped.
- 2 sticks celery finely sliced.
- 450g floury potatoes, chopped.
- 1 large carrot, chopped.
- 100g frozen peas
- 1 x 400g tin chopped tomatoes.
- 125g small pasta shapes
- 200g French beans, halved.
- quarter Savoy cabbage, chopped.
- 4 tbsp pesto sauce
- freshly ground pepper
- 1.5L vegetable stock
- 30g fresh Parmesan cheese shavings

INSTRUCTIONS

- Heat the oil in a large pan and add garlic, onion, carrot, celery, and potatoes. Fry for 3–4 minutes, until the vegetables soften but not brown.
- Add the water and tomatoes, bring to a boil, then lower the heat and let it cook for 10 minutes.
- Add the pasta, beans, peas, and carrots and cook for another 10 minutes or until the pasta is done.
- Mix in the parsley and pesto and add salt and pepper to taste. Serve with shaved Parmesan cheese on top.

NUTRIENTS (PER SERVINGS)

Carbs:40.7g | Fiber: 8.1g | Protein: 10.0g | Fat: 9.5g | Sugar: 9.4g

6. PUMPKIN SOUP

Servings: 4   Duration: 25 minutes

INGREDIENTS

- 1 tbsp olive oil
- Plain Greek yogurt (optional, for garnish)
- 2 cloves garlic, minced.
- 4 cups low-sodium vegetable broth
- 1 tsp ground cumin
- 1/2 tsp ground cinnamon
- 1 small onion, diced.
- 1 small pumpkin, peeled and diced (about 4 cups)
- 1/4 tsp ground nutmeg
- Salt and pepper to taste
- Fresh parsley or chives, chopped

INSTRUCTIONS

1. In a large saucepan, heat the olive oil over medium heat. Add onion, garlic, and sauté until tender.
2. Add pumpkin, water, cumin, cinnamon, and nutmeg. Simmer for 20 minutes or until pumpkin is soft. Turn off the heat.
3. Let the soup slightly cool down, then blend it with a hand blender until smooth.
4. Bring the pureed soup to the pan and heat it on low-medium heat. Add salt and pepper to taste.
5. Pour it into bowls. Add Greek yogurt and fresh parsley or onions, if desired.
6. Serve hot and have fun!

NUTRIENTS (PER SERVINGS)

Carbs: 20g | Protein: 5g | Fat: 3g | Fiber: 5g | Sugar: 8g | Sodium: 200mg

7. WHITE BEAN SOUP

Servings: 4-5   Duration: 30 minutes

INGREDIENTS	INSTRUCTIONS
<ul><li>1 tsp dried thyme</li><li>1 onion finely chopped.</li><li>2 cloves garlic, minced.</li><li>1 tbsp olive oil</li><li>2 celery stalks, diced.</li><li>4 cups low-sodium vegetable broth</li><li>2 carrots, diced.</li><li>2 cups cooked white beans.</li><li>1 bay leaf</li><li>Salt and pepper to taste</li><li>Fresh parsley for garnish</li></ul>	<ul><li>Take a large saucepan and heat the olive oil. Add onion and garlic and sauté until the onion is clear.</li><li>Celery and carrots should be cooked until they are soft.</li><li>Pour in the water, add the thyme, and bay leaf. Bring to a boil, lower the heat, and let it cook for 15 minutes.</li><li>Remove the bay leaf, add the cooked white beans, and keep cooking for an additional 10 minutes.</li><li>Puree a small amount of the soup to make it thick.</li><li>Add salt and pepper to taste.</li><li>Serve hot, with parsley on top.</li></ul>

NUTRIENTS (PER SERVINGS)

Carbs: 34g | Protein: 10g | Fat: 4g | Fiber: 8g | Sodium: 300mg

8. CREAMY BROCCOLI SOUP

Servings: 4   Duration: 20 minutes

INGREDIENTS	INSTRUCTIONS
<ul><li>1 tbsp olive oil</li><li>3 cups low-sodium vegetable broth</li><li>1 small onion, chopped.</li><li>2 cloves garlic, minced.</li><li>2 cups broccoli florets</li><li>1 cup unsweetened almond milk (or low-fat milk)</li><li>Salt and pepper to taste</li><li>Optional toppings: chopped almonds, grated Parmesan cheese, or plain Greek yogurt (in moderation)</li></ul>	1. Cook the broccoli florets until they are tender by either steaming or boiling them. 2. Heat olive oil in a pot and cook the onion and garlic until they become soft. 3. Add the cooked broccoli and vegetable broth to the pot, then let it simmer for 10 minutes. 4. Use a blender or food processor to blend the soup until it becomes smooth and creamy. 5. Return the soup to the heat, add almond milk (or low-fat milk), and warm it up. 6. Add salt and pepper to taste. 7. Serve the soup hot, and consider adding optional toppings such as almonds, Parmesan cheese, or Greek yogurt in moderation.

NUTRIENTS (PER SERVINGS)

Carbs: 10g | Protein: 4g | Fat: 6g | Fiber: 4g | Sodium: 300mg

. BUTTERNUT SQUASH SOUP

Servings: 5-6   Duration: 40 minutes

INGREDIENTS

- 1 cup unsweetened almond milk (or any other unsweetened non-dairy milk)
- 1 medium onion, chopped.
- 2 cloves garlic, minced.
- 1 tsp ground cinnamon
- 1 medium-sized butternut squash (about 2 pounds), peeled, seeded, and cubed.
- 1/2 tsp ground nutmeg
- Salt and pepper to taste
- Olive oil for cooking
- 2 cups low-sodium vegetable broth

INSTRUCTIONS

1. Add garlic and onion in olive oil over medium heat in a large pan, and sauté until the onion becomes transparent.
2. Add the cubed butternut squash and cook for 5 minutes.
3. Pour in the vegetable broth, cover, and let it cook on low for 20 to 25 minutes or until the squash is soft.
4. Blend the ingredients until smooth.
5. Stir in the almond milk, cinnamon, nutmeg, salt, and pepper. When you put it, turn on the heat to medium-low.
6. Cook for 5 minutes more.
7. Taste and adjust seasonings as desired. Serve hot and enjoy!

NUTRIENTS (PER SERVINGS)

Carbs: 20g | Fiber: 3g | Protein: 4g | Fat: 2g

0. LENTIL SOUP

Servings: 5   Duration: 40 minutes

INGREDIENTS

- 1 cup dried lentils
- 1 tsp ground turmeric
- 2 cloves garlic, minced.
- 1 small onion, chopped.
- 2 carrots, diced.
- 1 can (14.5 ounces) diced tomatoes (no added sugar)
- 2 celery stalks, diced.
- 4 cups low-sodium vegetable broth
- 1 tsp ground cumin
- 1/2 tsp paprika
- Salt and pepper to taste
- 1 Tbsp Olive oil

INSTRUCTIONS

1. Drizzle olive oil into a large pot over medium heat.
2. Add the onion and garlic. Sauté until transparent and aromatic.
3. Add the diced carrots and celery and simmer for 3–4 minutes, stirring regularly.
4. Add washed lentils, vegetable broth, chopped tomatoes (including juice), cumin, turmeric, paprika, salt, and pepper to the pot. Mix well.
5. Bring the mixture to a boil, then lower the heat, cover, and simmer for 30–40 minutes until the lentils are cooked. Stir occasionally.
6. Taste the soup once the lentils and veggies are soft and adjust the seasonings.
7. Remove from heat and let it cool slightly before serving.
8. Serve in your favorite dish. Garnish with parsley or lemon juice.

NUTRIENTS (PER SERVINGS)

Carbohydrates: 40g | Fiber: 15g | Protein: 12g | Fat: 4g

CHAPTER 7

POULTRY

1. Lemon Chicken Breast

2. Chicken Nuggets

3. Shredded Buffalo Chicken

4. Crispy Chicken Thighs

5. Chicken Masala

6. Thanksgiving Turkey Breast

7. Chicken Pot Pie

8. Turkey and Quinoa Caprese Casserole

9. Lemon-Pepper Chicken Wings

10. Teriyaki Turkey Meatballs

11. Baked Spaghetti with Ground Turkey

. LEMON CHICKEN BREAST

ervings: 4   Duration: 35 minutes

INGREDIENTS	INSTRUCTIONS
• 1 tbsp olive oil • 1-pound boneless chicken breast (4 pieces) • 1 tsp onion powder • 1 ½ tsp oregano powder • Cooking spray • ½ tsp salt & white pepper • I large lemon	1. Preheat oven to 375°F. 2. Spray one side of a large piece of aluminum foil with nonstick cooking spray. 3. Place four chicken breasts on the sprayed side of the foil. 4. Drizzle breasts with olive oil. Sprinkle lemon zest, white pepper, oregano, and onion powder. 5. Pour lemon juice over the chicken. Fold the foil to seal and create a packet. 6. Bake for 30 minutes. Open the foil carefully and transfer the chicken to your favorite serving plate. Enjoy!

NUTRIENTS (PER SERVINGS)

Carbs: 3g | Protein: 30g | Fat: 7g | Cholesterol: 96mg | Sodium: 347 mg | Fiber: 0g

. CHICKEN NUGGETS

ervings: 5   Duration: 40 minutes

INGREDIENTS	INSTRUCTIONS
• 1/2 garlic powder • 1 lb. boneless chicken breasts, cut into small bite pieces. • ½ tsp oregano, dried • 1/2 cup almond flour • Cooking spray • 1/4 tsp salt • 1 tsp paprika • 1/4 tsp black pepper • ½ tsp onion powder • 2 eggs • 1/4 cup grated Parmesan cheese	1. Preheat your oven to 400°F and prepare a baking sheet by lining it with parchment paper and spraying it with cooking spray. 2. Combine parmesan cheese, dried oregano, paprika, almond flour, garlic powder, onion powder, salt, and black pepper in a bowl. 3. Take pieces of chicken and dip them in beaten eggs, then coat them with the mixture of almond flour and spices. 4. Arrange the coated chicken on the prepared baking sheet and lightly spray them with cooking spray. 5. Bake for 15-20 minutes, flipping the chicken halfway through until it turns golden brown and fully cooked. 6. Serve hot with low-sugar dipping sauce.

NUTRIENTS (PER SERVINGS)

Cholesterol: 135mg | Sodium: 340mg | Carbs: 3g | Fiber: 1g | Sugars: 0.5g | Protein: 31g

3. SHREDDED BUFFALO CHICKEN

Servings: 4-5   Duration: 4 hours

INGREDIENTS	INSTRUCTIONS
• 1 1/2 lbs chicken breasts, boneless • 1/4 cup chicken broth • 1 tsp onion powder • 1/4 cup melted butter. • 1 tbsp Worcestershire sauce • 1 tsp garlic powder • 2 tbsp white vinegar • 1/2 tsp salt & black pepper • 1 cup buffalo hot sauce • 1/4 tsp cayenne pepper	1. Put the chicken into a slow cooker. 2. Mix melted butter, buffalo sauce, vinegar, garlic powder, Worcestershire sauce, salt, pepper, onion powder, and cayenne pepper in a bowl. 3. Pour the sauce over the chicken. 4. Add chicken broth to the slow cooker. Cook on low heat for 4-6 hours until the chicken becomes tender. 5. Use two forks to shred the chicken. Let the chicken soak in the sauce for 15-20 minutes on low heat. 6. Adjust the seasoning if desired. 7. You can serve the chicken on sandwiches, wraps, or as a topping for salads.

NUTRIENTS (PER SERVINGS)

Protein: 30g | Fat: 12g | Carbs: 4g | Sugar:1g

4. CRISPY CHICKEN THIGHS

Servings: 4   Duration: 40-45 minutes

INGREDIENTS	INSTRUCTIONS
• 4 chicken thighs, bone-in • 1/2 tsp salt • 1 tsp garlic powder • 1/4 tsp black pepper • 1 tsp paprika • 1 tbsp olive oil	1. Preheat the oven to 425°F (220°C). 2. Prepare a baking sheet by lining it with foil and applying a light coating of cooking spray. 3. Dry the chicken thighs and place them on the baking sheet. 4. Use a brush to coat the thighs with olive oil evenly. 5. Combine paprika, garlic powder, salt, and black pepper in a bowl. 6. Sprinkle the spice mixture over the chicken thighs. 7. Bake for 35-40 min or until the skin becomes crispy. Serve with low-carb vegetables.

NUTRIENTS (PER SERVINGS)

Protein: 25g | Fat: 18g | Carbs: 1g | Fiber: 1g | Sugars: 1g

5. CHICKEN MASALA

Servings: 4   Duration: 30 minutes

INGREDIENTS	INSTRUCTIONS
• 500g chicken breasts, boneless, cut into bite-sized pieces. • 2 tbsp olive oil • 1-inch ginger piece, grated • 2 green chilies, chopped. • 1/2 tsp turmeric powder • 1 onion, chopped. • 2 tsp ground coriander • 1 tsp ground cumin • 1 cup tomato puree • 1/2 tsp red chili powder • 3 garlic cloves, minced. • 1/2 tsp garam masala • Salt to taste	1. Heat some olive oil in a frying pan and cook the onions until they become light brown. Add garlic, ginger, and green chilies, and cook for 2 minutes. 2. Combine turmeric, coriander, red chili powder, cumin, and garam masala in a separate bowl. Then, add this mixture to the pan and cook for about 1 minute. 3. Now stir the chicken into the pan and simmer until golden brown. 4. Pour in the tomato puree, add salt to taste, and mix well. 5. Cover the pan and cook for 15-20 min until the chicken becomes tender. 6. Take off the lid and cook for 5 minutes to thicken the sauce. Serve it hot, along with steamed brown rice.

NUTRIENTS (PER SERVINGS)

Carbs: 8g Protein: 28g Fat: 10g Fiber: 2g Sugar: 4g

. THANKSGIVING TURKEY BREAST

Servings: 8   Duration: 50 minutes

INGREDIENTS	INSTRUCTIONS
• 1(2-3 pound) boneless turkey breast • 1 cup low-sodium chicken broth • 1 tsp dried rosemary • 1 tsp garlic powder • 2 tbsp olive oil • 1/2 tsp salt • 1/4 tsp black pepper • 1 tsp dried thyme • 2 tbsp unsalted butter (optional)	1. Preheat the oven to 350°F (175°C). 2. Coat the turkey breast with olive oil. 3. Mix thyme, rosemary garlic powder, salt, and black pepper in a small bowl. 4. Sprinkle seasoning blend on turkey breast. Put the turkey breast in a baking dish and pour chicken broth around it. 5. Cover with foil and roast until internal temp is 165°F (74°C). 6. Brush with unsalted butter and cook uncovered for 15 minutes for browning. Let it rest for 10 minutes before slicing. Serve and enjoy diabetic-friendly turkey breast.

NUTRIENTS (PER SERVINGS)

Cholesterol: 90mg | Sodium: 330mg | Carbs: 2g | Protein: 33g

7. CHICKEN POT PIE

Servings: 6   Duration: 1 hour 30 minutes

INGREDIENTS	INSTRUCTIONS
<ul><li>1 egg</li><li>2 carrots, diced.</li><li>1/2 cup unsalted butter, cubed.</li><li>1 tbsp olive oil</li><li>1 onion, chopped.</li><li>1 cup low-sodium chicken broth</li><li>2 celery stalks, diced.</li><li>2 cups cooked chicken breast, diced.</li><li>1/2 cup almond milk</li><li>2 garlic cloves, minced.</li><li>2 tbsp cornstarch</li><li>1 tsp dried thyme</li><li>1/2 tsp salt</li><li>1 cup mushrooms, sliced.</li><li>1/4 tsp black pepper</li><li>1 cup green beans</li></ul>	1. Preheat the oven to 350°F (175°C). 2. Combine coconut flour, almond flour, and salt in a bowl. Add chilled butter and egg and mix until the dough forms. Now wrap the dough in plastic wrap, and keep it in the refrigerator for 15-20 min. 3. In a skillet, heat olive oil. Sauté garlic and onions until they become translucent. Add carrots, celery, mushrooms, and green beans. Sauté for 5 min more. 4. Mix chicken broth, almond milk, cornstarch, thyme, salt, and pepper in a separate bowl. Add the mixture to the skillet and let it cook until the sauce is thick. 5. Remove from heat and add cooked chicken. 6. Take half of the chilled dough, roll it out, and place it in a 9-inch pie dish. Press it into the dish. 7. Stir in vegetable and chicken filling into the dish. 8. Fold out the remaining dough and place it on top of the filling. Properly close the edges. 9. Bake for 35-40 min, or the crust turns golden brown. 10. Allow it to cool slightly before serving.

NUTRIENTS (PER SERVINGS)

Carbs: 13g | Protein: 24g | Fat: 33g | Fiber: 5g | Sugar: 4g | Sodium: 450mg

8. TURKEY AND QUINOA CAPRESE CASSEROLE

Servings: 4   Duration: 60 minutes

INGREDIENTS	INSTRUCTIONS
<ul><li>1 lab ground turkey</li><li>1 tbsp olive oil</li><li>1 cup cooked quinoa</li><li>1 cup shredded mozzarella cheese</li><li>½ tsp dried oregano</li><li>2 cups cherry tomatoes, halved.</li><li>1/4 cup fresh basil leaves, chopped.</li><li>2 cloves garlic, minced.</li><li>Salt and pepper to taste</li></ul>	1. Preheat the oven to 375°F (190°C). 2. Heat olive oil over medium heat and sauté minced garlic in a skillet for 1 minute. 3. Add ground turkey to the skillet, season with salt, pepper, and dried oregano, and cook until browned. 4. Layer cooked quinoa and cooked turkey in a lightly greased casserole dish. 5. Place halved cherry tomatoes on top and sprinkle shredded mozzarella cheese. 6. Bake in the preheated oven for 25-30 minutes until the cheese is melted. 7. Remove from oven and sprinkle chopped basil leaves over the top.

NUTRIENTS (PER SERVINGS)

Carbs: 16g | Protein: 30g | Fat: 16g | Fiber: 3g | Sugar: 5g

. LEMON-PEPPER CHICKEN WINGS

Servings: 5   Duration: 40 minutes

INGREDIENTS

- 2 pounds (900g) chicken wings
- 1 tsp garlic powder
- 2 tbsp olive oil
- 1 tsp ground black pepper
- 2 tbsp fresh lemon juice
- 2 tbsp lemon zest
- 1/2 tsp salt
- Fresh parsley for garnish

INSTRUCTIONS

1. Preheat the oven to 400°F (200°C).
2. In a bowl, combine olive oil, lemon zest, garlic powder, lemon juice, black pepper, and salt (if desired).
3. Dry the chicken wings and put them in a large bowl.
4. Pour the lemon-pepper marinade over the wings, ensuring they are coated evenly. Allow them to marinate for 10 minutes.
5. Prepare a baking sheet by lining it with parchment paper and placing the wings in a single layer.
6. Bake for 30-35 minutes, flipping them halfway through, until the wings are thoroughly cooked and golden brown.
7. Garnish with fresh parsley and serve the wings hot.

NUTRIENTS (PER SERVINGS)

Carbs: 2g | Protein: 26g | Fat: 18g | Fiber: 0g | Sodium: 250mg

0. TERIYAKI TURKEY MEATBALLS

Servings: 4   Duration: 25 minutes

INGREDIENTS

- 1 lb ground turkey
- 1/4 cup low-sodium soy sauce
- 2 tbsp unsweetened apple juice
- 1/4 cup almond flour
- 1 tbsp sesame oil
- 1 tbsp grated fresh ginger.
- 2 tbsp rice vinegar
- 1/4 tsp black pepper
- Chopped green onions. (optional)
- 2 garlic cloves, minced. Sesame seeds for garnish (optional)

INSTRUCTIONS

- Preheat the oven to 375°F (190°C).
- Mix ground turkey, garlic, almond flour, ginger, and black pepper.
- Shape into 1-inch meatballs and bake for 15-18 minutes. Mix soy sauce, rice vinegar, apple juice, and sesame oil in a saucepan.
- Cook the mixture over low heat for 5 minutes until it thickens slightly.
- Pour the teriyaki sauce over the meatballs, garnish with green onions and sesame seeds (optional). Serve and enjoy!

NUTRIENTS (PER SERVINGS)

Protein: 24g | Fat: 12g | Carbohydrates: 6g | Fiber: 1g | Sugar: 2g | Sodium: 500mg

11. BAKED SPAGHETTI WITH GROUND TURKEY

Servings: 5   Duration: 55 minutes

INGREDIENTS	INSTRUCTIONS
<ul><li>8 oz whole wheat spaghetti</li><li>1 tsp dried basil</li><li>1 onion, chopped.</li><li>1 cup reduced-fat shredded mozzarella cheese.</li><li>2 garlic cloves, minced.</li><li>1 lb. lean ground turkey</li><li>1 can (8 oz) no-added-sugar tomato sauce</li><li>1 tsp dried oregano</li><li>1 can (14.5 oz) no-added-sugar diced tomatoes.</li><li>Salt and pepper to taste</li></ul>	1. Prepare the spaghetti as directed on the package, then strain it. 2. In a pan, cook ground turkey with onion and garlic until browned. 3. Combine tomato sauce, basil, diced tomatoes, oregano, salt, and pepper in the same pan. Let it simmer for 10 minutes. 4. Combine the cooked spaghetti with the sauce and place the mixture in a baking dish. 5. Sprinkle shredded mozzarella cheese on the top. 6. Bake the dish at 375°F for 20-25 minutes, until the cheese is melted.

NUTRIENTS (PER SERVINGS)

Carbs: 30g | Protein: 30g | Fat: 12g | Fiber: 6g

CHAPTER 8

BEEF & PORK

1. Bavarian Beef

2. Pork Chop Diane

3. Beef Stroganoff

4. Sage-Parmesan Pork Chops

5. Black Bean and Beef Steak Tacos

6. Cheddar-Beef Burger

7. Steak Gyro Platter

8. Grilled Pork Loin Chops

9. Mustard Herb Pork Tenderloin

10. Jalapeno Popper Pork Chops

BAVARIAN BEEF

Servings: 2   Duration: 2 hours

INGREDIENTS	INSTRUCTIONS
• 1.5 lb. lean beef, cubed. • 1 tsp dried thyme • 1 cup low-sodium beef broth • 2 tbsp tomato paste (no added sugar) • 1 onion, chopped. • 1 tbsp Dijon mustard • 2 garlic cloves, minced. • 1 tsp paprika • Salt and pepper, to taste. • 2 tbsp olive oil • 2 tbsp flour (low-carb alternative, if desired)	• Mix beef in a shallow bowl with onion, garlic, salt, olive oil, paprika, thyme, and pepper. Keep the marinade in the freezer for 1 hour. • Next, heat a skillet and brown the marinated beef. Set it aside. • Using the same skillet, cook flour for 1-2 min. Then, stir in beef broth, tomato paste, and Dijon mustard. • Put the browned beef back into the skillet, add bay leaves, and bring the mixture to a boil. • Once boiling, reduce the heat, cover the skillet, and let it simmer for 1.5 to 2 hours until the beef becomes tender. Stir occasionally. • Add salt and pepper to taste. Remove the bay leaves and garnish with parsley.

NUTRIENTS (PER SERVINGS)

Cholesterol: 80mg | Sodium: 400mg | Carbs: 20g | Fiber: 4g | Sugars: 8g |

PORK CHOP DIANE

Servings: 4   Duration: 30 minutes

INGREDIENTS	INSTRUCTIONS
• 4 boneless pork chops (4 oz each) 1/4 cup low-sodium chicken broth 2 tbsp lemon juice • 2 tbsp chopped fresh parsley. • 2 tbsp olive oil 2 garlic cloves, minced. 1/2 tsp dried thyme 1 tbsp Worcestershire Sauce 1 tbsp Dijon mustard 1/2 tsp black pepper	• Preheat oven to 375°F (190°C). • Mix olive oil, Worcestershire sauce, lemon juice, thyme, garlic, and black pepper in a bowl. • Marinate pork chops in the mixture for 10 minutes. • Sear pork chops in a skillet over medium-high heat for 2 min on both sides. • Transfer skillet to oven and bake for 8-10 minutes at 375°F (190°C). • Simmer reserved marinade, chicken broth, and Dijon mustard in a saucepan for 3-4 minutes. • Rest cooked pork chops, then drizzle with the sauce and garnish with parsley.

NUTRIENTS (PER SERVINGS)

Carbs: 2g | Protein: 26g | Fat: 16g | Fiber: 0.5g | Sodium: 200mg

3. BEEF STROGANOFF

Servings: 4   Duration: 40 minutes

INGREDIENTS	INSTRUCTIONS
• 1 tbsp olive oil • 8 oz. (225g) mushrooms, sliced. • 1/2 cup low-fat plain Greek yogurt • 1 onion, sliced. • 1 lb. (450g) lean beef thinly sliced. • 1 tbsp Dijon mustard • 2 garlic cloves, minced. • 4 cups cooked whole wheat egg noodles or zucchini noodles. • 1 tbsp reduced-sugar Worcestershire sauce. • Salt and pepper, to taste. • 1 cup reduced-sodium beef broth	1. Brown the beef in a skillet with olive oil, then set it aside. 2. Sauté onion and garlic in the same beef skillet until translucent. 3. Add mushrooms and cook until tender. 4. Pour in beef broth, Dijon mustard, and Worcestershire sauce. Simmer for 5 minutes to boil, then reduce the heat. 5. Return beef to the skillet and cook for 2-3 min more. 6. Remove from heat and stir in Greek yogurt. Season with salt and pepper. 7. Serve over whole wheat egg noodles or zucchini noodles.

NUTRIENTS (PER SERVINGS)

Carbs: 18g | Protein: 30g | Fat: 15g | Fiber: 3g | Sodium: 380mg

4. SAGE-PARMESAN PORK CHOPS

Servings: 4   Duration: 30 minutes

INGREDIENTS	INSTRUCTIONS
• 2 tbsp olive oil • 1/4 cup grated Parmesan cheese. • 1 tbsp dried sage • 4 boneless pork chops (4 oz each) • Salt and pepper to taste	1. Preheat the oven to 375°F (190°C). 2. Add salt, pepper, and dried sage to the pork chops for seasoning. 3. In a pan, heat olive oil over medium-high heat. 4. Cook the pork chops on each side for 2-3 minutes until they are brown. 5. Transfer the pork chops to a baking dish and sprinkle them with Parmesan cheese. 6. Bake the pork chops at 375°F (190°C) for approx. 15 min, or until their internal temp reaches 145°F (63°C). Serve hot with your favorite toppings and enjoy healthy eating!

NUTRIENTS (PER SERVINGS)

Fat: 14g | Cholesterol: 75mg | Sodium: 220mg | Carbs: 1g | Sugars: 1g | Protein: 29g

5. BLACK BEAN AND BEEF STEAK TACOS

Servings: 4   Duration: 30 minutes

INGREDIENTS	INSTRUCTIONS
• 1 lb. (450g) lean beef steak thinly sliced. • 1 tbsp olive oil • 1 cup canned black beans, rinsed and drained. • 8 small corn tortillas • 1 tsp ground cumin • 1 bell pepper thinly sliced. • Fresh cilantro (for garnish) • 2 cloves garlic, minced. • 1 tsp chili powder • 1 onion, sliced. • Salt and pepper to taste • Lime wedges (for serving)	1. Preheat the oven to 350°F (175°C) to prepare the dish and warm the tortillas in foil. 2. Brown the sliced beef steak in a pan over low-medium heat, then set it aside. 3. In the same pan, sauté the sliced onion, bell pepper, and minced garlic until tender. 4. Add the cooked steak to the pan with the 5. vegetables. Add chili powder, ground cumin, salt, and pepper, stirring to coat everything. 6. Cook for an extra 2-3 min to let the flavors meld. 7. Add rinsed black beans and cook for another 2-3 minutes. 8. Remove the warmed tortillas from the oven and fill them with the black bean and beef steak mixture. Garnish with cilantro and serve with lime wedges.

NUTRIENTS (PER SERVINGS)

Carbs: 41g | Fiber: 10g | Sugars: 4g | Protein: 33g | Sodium: 320mg

. CHAEDDAR-BEEF BURGER

Servings: 4   Duration: 25 minutes

INGREDIENTS	INSTRUCTIONS
• 4 slices reduced-fat cheddar cheese. • 1 lb. lean ground beef (90% lean) • 1/2 tsp salt • 4 whole wheat burger buns • Mustard and sugar-free ketchup (optional) • Lettuce, tomato slices, and red onion for toppings • 1/4 tsp black pepper	1. Heat grill or stovetop grill pan to medium-high temp. 2. In a large bowl, combine ground beef with salt and black pepper, and form the mixture into 4 patties. 3. Grill the patties for approx. 4-5 min on each side. 4. When the burgers are almost done, place a slice of reduced-fat cheddar cheese on top of each patty and let it melt for 1 minute. 5. Toast whole wheat burger buns lightly. 6. Arrange the burgers by adding lettuce, tomato, red onion, and optionally mustard or ketchup. 7. Serve immediately and enjoy your meal!

NUTRIENTS (PER SERVINGS)

Carbs: 28g | Fiber: 5g | Sugar: 5g | Protein: 35g | Sodium: 320mg

7. STEAK GYRO PLATTER

Servings: 4   Duration: 40 minutes

INGREDIENTS	INSTRUCTIONS
<ul><li>4 whole wheat pitas</li><li>1 lb. lean beef steak</li><li>1 cucumber, diced.</li><li>2 tbsp olive oil</li><li>1 tsp dried oregano</li><li>2 garlic cloves, minced.</li><li>Fresh lettuce or spinach leaves</li><li>1 small red onion thinly sliced.</li><li>Salt and pepper to taste</li><li>1 cup plain Greek yogurt.</li><li>1 tomato, diced.</li><li>1 tbsp fresh lemon juice</li></ul>	1. Assemble garlic, olive oil, oregano, pepper, and salt in a bowl. Rub the spice mixture on the steak well and let it sit for at least 20 minutes. 2. Grill the steak for 4-6 minutes per side until cooked to your liking. Slice the steaks thinly after 5 min wait. 3. Mix lemon juice, Greek yogurt, salt, and pepper to make the sauce. 4. Warm the whole wheat pitas in a skillet or oven. 5. Spread yogurt sauce on each pita, then add sliced steak, cucumber, red onion, tomato, and lettuce or spinach. 6. Serve the steak gyro platter with extra yogurt sauce.

NUTRIENTS (PER SERVINGS)

Carbs: 33g | Protein: 32g | Fat: 14g | Fiber: 6g | Sodium: 265mg

8. GRILLED PORK LOIN CHOPS

Servings: 4   Duration: 45 minutes

INGREDIENTS	INSTRUCTIONS
<ul><li>2 tbsp low-sodium soy sauce</li><li>1 tsp dried oregano</li><li>4 pork loin chops (4 oz each)</li><li>2 tbsp fresh lemon juice</li><li>2 tbsp olive oil</li><li>Cooking spray</li><li>2 cloves garlic, minced.</li><li>1/2 tsp black pepper</li></ul>	1. Add olive oil, lemon juice, dried oregano, soy sauce, minced garlic, and black pepper in a shallow pot, and mix well to make the marinade. 2. Apply the marinade to the pork chops, and place them in the freezer for 30 min. 3. Preheat the grill and lightly spray the grates with cooking spray. 4. Grill pork chops on each side for 6-8 minutes until the internal temperature reaches 145°F (63°C). Turn it off when it turns crispy and tender. 5. Allow the pork chops to rest before serving.

NUTRIENTS (PER SERVINGS)

Cholesterol: 80mg | Sodium: 350mg | Carbohydrates: 2g | Fiber: 0g | Sugar: 0g | Protein: 29g

. MUSTARD HERB PORK TENDERLOIN

Servings: 4   Duration: 30 minutes

INGREDIENTS

- 1 lb. pork tenderloin
- 1 garlic clove, minced.
- 1 tbsp olive oil
- 1 tbsp fresh chopped herbs (e.g., thyme, rosemary, sage)
- 2 tbsp sugar-free Dijon mustard
- Salt and pepper to taste

INSTRUCTIONS

1. Preheat the oven to 375°F (190°C).
2. Mix garlic, olive oil, mustard, herbs, salt, and pepper in a bowl.
3. Apply the mustard herb paste evenly over the entire surface of the tenderloin using a hand or spoon.
4. Put the tenderloin on a baking sheet or in a roasting pan.
5. Place the pork tenderloin in the oven, and roast for 20-25 minutes until the meat becomes tender.
6. Allow it to rest for a few minutes, then slice and serve.
7. Enjoy with low-carb veggies.

NUTRIENTS (PER SERVINGS)

Cholesterol: 74mg | Sodium: 280mg | Total Carbohydrates: 1g | Protein: 26g

0. JALAPENO POPPER PORK CHOPS

Servings: 6   Duration: 40 minutes

INGREDIENTS

- 6 boneless pork chops
- 1/4 cup grated Parmesan cheese.
- 1/2 tsp paprika
- 4 jalapeno peppers seeded and diced.
- 1/4 cup shredded cheddar cheese (reduced-fat option if desired)
- 1 tsp garlic powder
- 4 oz. softened cream cheese (low-fat option if desired)
- 1/4 cup almond flour
- Salt and pepper, to taste.
- Cooking spray

INSTRUCTIONS

1. Preheat your oven to 375°F (190°C).
2. In a bowl, combine cream cheese, jalapenos, and cheddar cheese.
3. Cut a pocket in each pork chop and fill it with the cream cheese mixture.
4. Mix almond flour, garlic powder, paprika, Parmesan cheese, salt, and pepper in another bowl.
5. Coat the pork chops with the almond flour mixture.
6. Grease a baking dish and place the coated pork chops in it.
7. Bake the pork chops in the preheated oven for 25-30 minutes at 375°F (190°C) until fully cooked.
8. Once cooked, remove the pork chops from the oven. You can add a garnish of fresh cilantro and serve them with lime wedges. (optional)

NUTRIENTS (PER SERVINGS)

Carbs: 5g | Protein: 31g | Fat: 20g | Fiber: 1g | Sugar: 2g

CHAPTER 9

FISH & SEAFOOD

1. Seafood Risotto

2. Trout with Basil Sauce

3. Caprese Shrimp Pasta

4. Cod with Mango Salsa

5. Sole Piccata

6. Catfish with Corn and Pepper Relish

7. Blackened Salmon

8. Aromatic Mackerel

9. Tuna Poke with Riced Broccoli

10. Baked Cod with Tomatoes and Olives

SEAFOOD RISOTTO

Servings: 4   Duration: 40 minutes

INGREDIENTS	INSTRUCTIONS
<ul><li>1 tbsp olive oil</li><li>1 cup mixed seafood (shrimp, scallops, mussels), cleaned.</li><li>1 small onion finely chopped.</li><li>1 cup Arborio rice (risotto rice)</li><li>2 tbsp chopped fresh parsley.</li><li>4 cups low-sodium chicken or vegetable broth</li><li>1/2 cup diced tomatoes.</li><li>1/4 cup grated Parmesan cheese.</li><li>2 garlic cloves, minced.</li><li>Salt and pepper</li></ul>	1. Heat olive oil in a large saucepan and sauté chopped onion and minced garlic for 3-4 minutes. 2. Add Arborio rice and stir to coat with oil, cooking for an additional 2 minutes. 3. Gradually add chicken or vegetable broth, stirring constantly, and let the rice absorb the liquid before adding more. Cook for 20-25 minutes until the rice becomes tender. 4. In a separate skillet, sauté mixed seafood until fully cooked, then set it aside. 5. Combine the cooked seafood and diced tomatoes with the rice, gently stirring to mix them. 6. Remove from heat and add grated Parmesan cheese. Season with salt and pepper. 7. Serve immediately, garnished with freshly chopped parsley.

NUTRIENTS (PER SERVINGS)

Carbs: 40g | Protein: 15g | Fat: 8g | Fiber: 2g | Sodium: 450mg

TROUT WITH BASIL SAUCE

Servings: 3   Duration: 50 minutes

INGREDIENTS	INSTRUCTIONS
<ul><li>4 (8-ounce) trout fillets, skinless</li><li>2 tbsp olive oil</li><li>1 clove garlic</li><li>1/4 cup grated Parmesan cheese (optional)</li><li>Salt and pepper, to taste.</li><li>1/4 cup extra virgin olive oil.</li><li>2 cups fresh basil leaves</li><li>1/4 cup pine nuts</li></ul>	1. Preheat your oven to 375°F (190°C). 2. Add salt and pepper to the trout fillets. 3. Heat the olive oil in a skillet over medium heat. Sauté the trout fillets for 2-3 minutes on each side. 4. Place the cooked fillets onto a baking sheet and bake them in the preheated oven for about 8-10 min until fully cooked. 5. Use a food processor to combine basil leaves, garlic, pine nuts, and Parmesan cheese (optional). Pulse the mixture. 6. While the food processor runs, gradually pour in the olive oil until the sauce becomes smooth. 7. Add salt and pepper to the basil sauce for seasoning. Take the trout out of the oven and serve with the basil sauce spooned on top.

NUTRIENTS (PER SERVINGS)

Cholesterol: 75mg | Sodium: 150mg | Carbs: 1g | Sugars: 1g | Protein: 26g

3. CAPRESE SHRIMP PASTA

Servings: 6   Duration: 30 minutes

INGREDIENTS	INSTRUCTIONS
• 8 oz whole wheat or gluten-free pasta • 1/4 cup fresh basil leaves, torn. • 1 lb. shrimp peeled and deviated. • 2 garlic cloves, minced. • 8 oz fresh mozzarella cheese, diced. • 2 tbsp olive oil • Salt and pepper to taste • 2 cups cherry tomatoes, halved	1. Prepare the pasta as directed on the package, then strain and keep it aside. 2. Heat some olive oil and sauté minced garlic in a frying pan for a minute. 3. Add the shrimp to the pan and cook them for 3-4 minutes until they turn pink. Take out the shrimp and set them aside. 4. Using the same pan, cook the cherry tomatoes for 2-3 minutes until they become soft. Season them with salt and pepper. 5. Place the shrimp back into the pan, add the cooked pasta, and mix them together. 6. Remove the pan from heat and add diced mozzarella cheese. Gently stir the mixture to melt the cheese slightly. 7. Sprinkle torn basil leaves on top for garnish and serve promptly.

NUTRIENTS (PER SERVINGS)
Carbs: 35g | Protein: 30g | Fat: 16g | Fiber: 6g | Sugar: 4g | Sodium: 400mg

4. COD WITH MANGO SALSA

Servings: 2   Duration: 30 minutes

INGREDIENTS	INSTRUCTIONS
• 2 cod fillets (6 oz. each) • 1/4 red onion finely chopped. • 1 small jalapeno seeded and finely chopped. • 1 ripe mango, diced. • Juice of 1 lime • 1/4 cup fresh cilantro, chopped. • 1 tbsp olive oil • Salt and pepper, to taste	1. Preheat the oven to 400°F (200°C). 2. Sprinkle salt and pepper on the cod fillets. 3. In an oven-safe skillet, heat olive oil over medium-high heat. 4. Cook the cod fillets on each side for 2-3 minutes until they become lightly browned. 5. Move the skillet to the preheated oven and bake for about 8-10 minutes until the fish easily flakes apart. 6. Mix diced mango, red onion, jalapeno, cilantro, lime juice, salt, and pepper in a bowl. Stir the mix. 7. Take the cod out of the oven and serve the cod with the mango salsa on top.

NUTRIENTS (PER SERVINGS)

Carbs: 23g | Protein: 30g | Fat: 8g | Fiber: 3g | Sugar: 17g | Sodium: 90mg

5. SOLE PICCATA

Servings: 1   Duration: 10 minutes

INGREDIENTS	INSTRUCTIONS
• 1 sole fillet (4 ounces) • 1 tbsp chopped fresh parsley. • 1 tbsp lemon juice • 1 tbsp capers, drained • 1 tbsp olive oil • Salt and pepper to taste	1. Heat olive oil in a non-stick skillet on medium flame. 2. Sprinkle salt and pepper on both sides of the sole fillet. 3. Place the seasoned fillet in the skillet and cook it on each side for 2-3 minutes until it turns brown and cooks through. 4. Take the fillet out of the skillet and keep it aside. 5. Using the same skillet, add lemon juice and capers, stirring them for about 1 minute. 6. Put the sole fillet back into the skillet and ensure it gets coated with the lemon-caper sauce. Cook for another minute. 7. Transfer the cooked fish to a serving plate and garnish it with parsley. Serve immediately!

NUTRIENTS (PER SERVINGS)

Carbs: 1g | Protein: 28g | Fat: 11g | Fiber: 0g

6. CATFISH WITH CORN AND PEPPER RELISH

Servings: 4   Duration: 30 minutes

INGREDIENTS	INSTRUCTIONS
• 2 cups corn kernels • 1 red bell pepper, diced. • 4 (6-ounce) catfish fillets • 1 green bell pepper, diced. • 2 cloves garlic, minced. • 1 tbsp fresh cilantro, chopped. • 2 tbsp apple cider vinegar • 1 small red onion, diced. • Salt and pepper (to taste) • 1 tbsp lime juice	1. Sprinkle salt and pepper on catfish fillets, then cook them in the oven at 400°F (200°C) for 15-20 minutes. 2. In a frying pan, cook corn, red and green bell peppers, and red onion until they become slightly tender. 3. Add minced garlic and cook for one more minute. 4. Take the pan off the heat and mix in apple cider vinegar, lime juice, and cilantro. Season with salt and pepper. 5. Serve the baked catfish with the corn and pepper relish on top. Optionally, add more cilantro as a garnish. Enjoy your meal!

NUTRIENTS (PER SERVINGS)

Carbs: 25g | Protein: 25g | Fat: 10-15g | Fiber: 4g

7. BLACKENED SALMON

Servings: 1   Duration: 15-20 minutes

INGREDIENTS	INSTRUCTIONS
• 1 salmon fillet (4-6 ounces) • 1/2 tsp dried thyme • 1 tsp paprika • 1/2 tsp onion powder • 1/4 tsp salt (optional) • 1 tbsp olive oil • 1/2 tsp garlic powder • 1/4 tsp cayenne pepper • Lemon wedges	• Combine paprika, garlic powder, onion powder, dried thyme, black pepper, cayenne pepper, and salt in a small bowl. • Apply olive oil to the salmon. • Evenly distribute the spice mix over the salmon. • In a preheated skillet over medium-high heat, cook the salmon on each side for 4-5 minutes until fully cooked. • Allow the salmon to rest for a minute. Serve with lemon wedges. (optional)

NUTRIENTS (PER SERVINGS)

Protein: 25g | Fat: 15g | Carbs: 3g | Fiber: 1g | Sodium: Varies (depends on salt usage)

8. AROMATIC MACKEREL

Servings: 2   Duration: 25 minutes

INGREDIENTS	INSTRUCTIONS
• 2 fresh mackerel fillets • 1/2 tsp each paprika and cinnamon • 2 garlic cloves, grated. • 1 tsp each ground cumin, coriander, and turmeric • Fresh cilantro or parsley (for garnish) • 1 tbsp olive oil • Salt and pepper to taste • Lemon wedges (for serving)	1. Preheat your oven to 400°F (200°C). 2. Take a baking sheet and line it with parchment paper. 3. Put the mackerel fillets on the lined baking sheet. 4. Mix minced garlic, spices, salt, and pepper in a bowl. 5. Drizzle olive oil over the fillets and sprinkle the spice blend on top. 6. Place the baking sheet in the oven and bake for 15-18 minutes, or until the fish easily flakes with a fork. 7. Serve the mackerel hot, garnished with cilantro or parsley and lemon wedges.

NUTRIENTS (PER SERVINGS)

Carbs: 2g | Protein: 30g | Fat: 20g | Fiber: 1g

. TUNA POKE WITH RICED BROCCOLI

ervings: 7   Duration: 25 minutes

INGREDIENTS	INSTRUCTIONS
• 2 lbs. fresh sushi-grade tuna, cubed. • 1 tsp ginger, grated. • 2 tbsp sesame oil • 2 tbsp rice vinegar • 1/2 cup diced avocado. • 1/4 tsp red pepper flakes (optional) • 5 cups riced broccoli. • 4 tbsp low-sodium soy sauce • 1/2 cup diced cucumber. • 1 tsp minced garlic • 1/4 cup sliced green onions. • 1 tbsp sesame seeds • 1 tbsp honey (or sugar substitute)	1. Combine soy sauce, sesame oil, rice vinegar, honey, ginger, garlic, and red pepper flakes. 2. Add tuna and let it soak for 10 minutes in the fridge. 3. Grate or process broccoli until it looks like rice grains. 4. Cook the riced broccoli in a skillet for 5 minutes over medium heat. 5. Mix tuna, cucumber, avocado, and green onions in a bowl. 6. Separate the riced broccoli into 7 portions and place the tuna mixture on top of each. 7. Sprinkle sesame seeds over each serving. 8. Serve and savor!

NUTRIENTS (PER SERVINGS)

Carbs: 10g | Protein: 34g | Fat: 9g | Fiber: 5g | Sugars: 4g

0. BAKED COD WITH TOMATOES AND OLIVES

ervings: 1   Duration: 30 minutes

INGREDIENTS	INSTRUCTIONS
• 1 cod fillet (4-6 ounces) • 1 tbsp fresh lemon juice • 1 tsp olive oil 1/2 cup cherry tomatoes, halved. 1/2 tsp dried oregano 1/4 cup pitted olives, sliced. 1 clove garlic, minced. Salt and pepper to taste Fresh parsley for garnish	1. Preheat the oven to 375 degrees Fahrenheit (190 degrees Celsius). 2. Combine tomatoes, olives, garlic, lemon juice, olive oil, oregano, salt, and pepper in a bowl. 3. Put the cod fillet in a baking dish and evenly spread the tomato mixture on top. 4. Bake for 15-20 minutes until the fish becomes opaque and easily flakes apart. 5. Let it rest for a minute, then sprinkle with parsley as a garnish. 6. Serve alongside steamed vegetables or a salad.

NUTRIENTS (PER SERVINGS)

Calories: 220 | Carbs: 7g | Protein: 28g | Fat: 9g | Fiber: 3g

CHAPTER 10

VEGETABLES AND SIDE DISHES

1. Apple-Carrot Salad

2. Feta Spinach Salad

3. Easy Mashed Cauliflower

4. Chickpeas with Spinach

5. Heirloom Tomato Salad

6. Broccoli Salad

7. Lemon-Garlic Mushrooms

8. Zucchini Sauté

9. Broccoli with Pine Nuts

10. Fennel and Chickpeas

. APPLE-CARROT SALAD

ervings: 5   Duration: 15 minutes

INGREDIENTS	INSTRUCTIONS
• 2 tbsp lemon juice • 1/4 cup walnuts, chopped. • 2 medium-sized apples • 1/4 cup raisins (optional) • 1/2 tsp cinnamon (optional), • 3 medium-sized carrots • 1/4 cup plain Greek yogurt, • 1 tbsp honey (optional), • fresh mint leaves for garnish.	1. Mix grated carrots, diced apples, walnuts, lemon juice, and raisins, if desired, in a bowl. 2. Combine Greek yogurt, honey, and cinnamon in another bowl until thoroughly mixed. 3. Drizzle the yogurt dressing over the mixture of apples and carrots and gently toss. 4. Let it cool in the refrigerator for 10 minutes. 5. Serve in separate bowls and optionally decorate with mint leaves.

NUTRIENTS (PER SERVINGS)

Carbs: 15g | Fiber: 3g | Protein: 2g | Fat: 4g | Sodium: 20mg | Sugar: 9g

. FETA SPINACH SALAD

ervings: 4   Duration: 10 minutes

INGREDIENTS	INSTRUCTIONS
• 1 cup cherry tomatoes, halved. • 1/4 red onion thinly sliced. • 1/4 cup crumbled feta cheese (low-fat if preferred) 1 tbsp balsamic vinegar 6 cups fresh baby spinach • 1 tsp Dijon mustard 1/2 cucumber, sliced. 1 garlic clove, minced. Salt and pepper to taste 1/4 cup toasted pine nuts 2 tbsp extra-virgin olive oil	1. Cleanse and pat dry the spinach and cherry tomatoes. 2. Mix spinach and cherry tomatoes with cucumber and red onion. 3. Prepare the dressing in a separate bowl using olive oil, Dijon mustard, balsamic vinegar, salt, garlic, and pepper. 4. Pour the dressing over the salad and toss it together. 5. Add feta cheese and nuts as a final touch. You can serve the salad immediately or refrigerate it before serving.

NUTRIENTS (PER SERVINGS)

Carbs: 9g | Fiber: 3g | Protein: 5g | Fat: 11g | Sodium: 200mg

3. EASY MASHED CAULIFLOWER

Servings: 3   Duration: 20 minutes

INGREDIENTS	INSTRUCTIONS
• 1 tbsp olive oil • 1/4 cup low-fat milk • 1 medium cauliflower • 2 garlic cloves, minced. • Salt and pepper to taste • 2 tbsp unsalted butter • Optional: fresh herbs for topping	1. Wash and cut cauliflower into florets. Boil florets for 10-12 minutes. Drain well. 2. Heat olive oil. Sauté garlic for 1-2 minutes. 3. Now, transfer the cauliflower to a food processor. Add the sautéed garlic, butter, and milk to the processor. 4. Blend until smooth. Adjust the thickness by adding more milk. Season with salt and pepper. 5. Garnish with herbs for more flavor.

NUTRIENTS (PER SERVINGS)

Carbs: 7g | Fiber: 3g | Protein: 3g | Fat: 6g

4. CHICKPEAS WITH SPINACH

Servings: 4   Duration: 20 minutes

INGREDIENTS	INSTRUCTIONS
• 1 tbsp olive oil • 1 small onion finely chopped. • 1 can (14 oz) chickpeas, drained • 1/2 tsp turmeric • 2 cloves garlic, minced. • 1/4 tsp cayenne pepper (optional) • 1 can (14 oz) diced tomatoes (no sugar added) • 1 tsp ground cumin • 4 cups fresh spinach leaves • Salt and pepper to taste • 1 tsp ground coriander • 1/2 tsp paprika	1. Warm olive oil in a skillet over medium heat. 2. Sauté onion and garlic until tender (around 3-4 min). 3. Add cumin, coriander, turmeric, paprika, and optionally cayenne pepper, stirring for approximately 1 minute. 4. Stir in chickpeas and diced tomatoes into the pan; stir well. 5. Cover the skillet and let the mixture simmer for 10 minutes. 6. Finally, add spinach leaves and continue cooking until wilted (a few minutes). 7. Season with salt and pepper. Transfer the prepared dish to a serving plate and savor the flavors!

NUTRIENTS (PER SERVINGS)

Carbs: 31g | Fiber: 9g | Protein: 10g | Fat: 6g | Sodium: 303mg

5. HEIRLOOM TOMATO SALAD

Servings: 2   Duration: 10 minutes

INGREDIENTS	INSTRUCTIONS
<ul><li>1 medium-sized cucumber</li><li>1/4 cup fresh basil leaves</li><li>1 tbsp extra-virgin olive oil</li><li>2 heirloom tomatoes</li><li>1 tbsp balsamic vinegar</li><li>1/4 red onion</li><li>Salt and pepper to taste</li></ul>	1. Wash tomatoes, cucumber, and basil. Pat dry. 2. Slice tomatoes and place on a plate. Cut the cucumber into rounds and arrange on top. 3. Thinly slice red onion, sprinkle over tomatoes and cucumber. 4. Tear basil leaves and scatter on the salad. 5. Whisk olive oil and balsamic vinegar in a bowl for dressing. 6. Drizzle dressing over salad, season with salt and pepper. Let sit for 10 mins to meld flavors. 7. Serve Heirloom Tomato Salad as a side dish or light meal.

NUTRIENTS (PER SERVINGS)

Carbs: 9g | Fiber: 2g | Fat: 7g | Protein: 2g

6. BROCCOLI SALAD

Servings: 4   Duration: 15 minutes

INGREDIENTS	INSTRUCTIONS
<ul><li>2 cups fresh broccoli florets</li><li>2 tbsp unsweetened dried cranberries</li><li>1 tsp Dijon mustard</li><li>1/4 cup chopped unsalted walnuts or almonds.</li><li>2 tbsp low-fat plain yoghurt</li><li>1/4 cup diced red onion.</li><li>1 tbsp apple cider vinegar</li><li>Salt and pepper to taste</li></ul>	1. Steam or blanch the broccoli florets until they are cooked. Remove from heat and allow them to cool. 2. Mix the red onion, cranberries, cooked broccoli, and nuts in a bowl. 3. Whisk together the apple cider vinegar, Dijon mustard, yogurt, salt, and pepper in another bowl. 4. Drizzle the dressing over the broccoli mixture and mix well to ensure everything is coated. 5. Place the bowl in the refrigerator for at least 1 hour before you serve it.

NUTRIENTS (PER SERVINGS)

Carbs: 10g | Fiber: 3g | Protein: 4g | Fat: 6g | Sodium: 75mg

7. LEMON-GARLIC MUSHROOMS

Servings: 4   Duration: 25 minutes

INGREDIENTS	INSTRUCTIONS
<ul><li>1 lb. mushrooms, sliced.</li><li>1 tsp lemon zest</li><li>2 tbsp lemon juice</li><li>2 tbsp olive oil</li><li>1/4 tsp black pepper</li><li>4 cloves garlic, minced.</li><li>2 tbsp fresh parsley (optional)</li><li>1/4 tsp salt</li></ul>	1. Heat olive oil in a skillet over medium heat. Sauté minced garlic until it becomes fragrant. 2. Add sliced mushrooms for approximately 5 minutes until they become soft. 3. Stir in lemon zest, lemon juice, salt, and black pepper, and cook for an additional 2-3 minutes. 4. Remove the skillet from the heat and transfer to a serving dish. Garnish with parsley. Serve as a side or used as a topping for chicken, fish, or vegetables.

NUTRIENTS (PER SERVINGS)

Carbs: 6g | Fat: 7g | Protein: 3g | Fiber: 2g | Sugar: 2g | Sodium: 150mg

8. ZUCCHINI SAUTÉ

Servings: 4   Duration: 15 minutes

INGREDIENTS	INSTRUCTIONS
<ul><li>1 medium onion thinly sliced.</li><li>Fresh parsley for garnish</li><li>2 garlic cloves, minced.</li><li>2 tbsp olive oil</li><li>4 medium zucchinis, sliced.</li><li>Salt, pepper, and red pepper flakes (optional)</li></ul>	1. Heat olive oil in a skillet over medium heat. 2. Sauté the onion and garlic until they release a pleasant aroma. 3. Add zucchini to the skillet and sprinkle it with salt, pepper, and red pepper flakes to enhance the flavor. 4. Continue sautéing for 5 to 7 minutes until tender. 5. Finally, top the dish with parsley and present it for serving.

NUTRIENTS (PER SERVINGS)

Carbs: 7g | Protein: 2g | Fat: 5g | Fiber: 2g | Sugar: 4g

. BROCCOLI WITH PINE NUTS

ervings: 2   Duration: 20 minutes

INGREDIENTS

- 2 garlic cloves, minced.
- 1 head broccoli, florets
- 2 tbsp pine nuts
- 2 tbsp olive oil
- Salt and pepper to taste

INSTRUCTIONS

1. Boil broccoli florets in boiling water until they are soft. Drain and keep them aside.
2. Heat olive oil and sauté minced garlic in a skillet until it becomes fragrant.
3. Add the broccoli to the skillet and cook it for 2-3 minutes until it becomes tender.
4. In a separate pan, toast the pine nuts until they turn golden brown.
5. Season the broccoli with salt and pepper, and gently toss it.
6. Transfer the broccoli to a serving dish and sprinkle the toasted pine nuts over the top.

NUTRIENTS (PER SERVINGS)

Carbs: 7g | Fiber: 3g | Sugars: 2g | Protein: 3g | Sodium: 25mg

0. FENNEL AND CHICKPEAS

ervings: 2   Duration: 25 minutes

INGREDIENTS

- 2 garlic cloves, minced.
- 1 tbsp olive oil
- 1 can (15 ounces) chickpeas drained and rinsed.
- 1 tsp ground cumin
- 2 fennel bulbs thinly sliced.
- 1 onion, chopped.
- 1/2 tsp turmeric
- Salt and pepper to taste
- 1 tsp ground coriander
- Fresh lemon juice (from 1/2 lemon)
- Fresh parsley, chopped (for garnish)

INSTRUCTIONS

1. In a pan, sauté diced onion and minced garlic in olive oil until softened.
2. Add sliced fennel bulbs and cook until they become tender.
3. Stir in chickpeas, turmeric, coriander, cumin, salt, and pepper. Mix well.
4. Place a lid on the pan and let it simmer for 10-15 minutes until the fennel is soft.
5. Squeeze some freshly squeezed lemon juice onto the dish and stir. Sprinkle with chopped parsley for garnishing. Serve and savor!

NUTRIENTS (PER SERVINGS)

Carbs: 29g | Fiber: 9g | Sugar: 4g | Protein: 9g | Sodium: 300mg

CHAPTER 11

SNACKS AND APPERTIZERS

1. Parmesan Zucchini Fries

2. Tuna Ceviche

3. Open Sardine Sandwich

4. Hummus

5. Fresh Dill Dip

6. Creamy Cheese Dip

7. Spinach and Artichoke Dip

8. No-Bake Coconut and Cashew Energy Bars

9. Cinnamon Toasted Pumpkin Seeds

10. Cucumber Pate

PARMESAN ZUCCHINI FRIES

Servings: 3-4   Duration: 35 minutes

INGREDIENTS	INSTRUCTIONS
• 2 medium zucchinis • 1 tsp dried oregano • 1/4 tsp black pepper • 1 tsp garlic powder • 1/4 cup grated Parmesan cheese. • 1/2 tsp paprika • 2 large eggs, beaten. • 1/4 cup almond flour • Cooking spray • 1/4 tsp salt	1. Preheat the oven to 425°F (220°C). Line a baking sheet with parchment paper. 2. Cut the zucchini French fries shaped. 3. Add almond flour, paprika, oregano, Parmesan cheese, garlic powder, salt, and pepper in a shallow dish. 4. Dip the zucchini sticks into beaten eggs, then cover them with the Parmesan mixture. 5. Arrange the coated zucchini fries on the baking sheet. Lightly coat of cooking spray. 6. Bake for approx. 15-20 min until they turn a golden brown. Serve immediately!

NUTRIENTS (PER SERVINGS)

Carbs: 8g | Fiber: 3g | Protein: 9g | Fat: 7g | Sodium: 380mg

TUNA CEVICHE

Servings: 2   Duration: 20-30 minutes

INGREDIENTS	INSTRUCTIONS
• 1/2 lb. tuna, sushi-grade • 1 tbsp extra-virgin olive oil • 1/2 red onion, sliced. • 1 jalapeño pepper, chopped. • 1/4 cup lime juice • Salt and pepper to taste • Cucumber slices (optional) ¼ lemon juice 2 tbsp fresh cilantro, chopped	1. Dice the tuna into small portions and place them in a bowl. 2. Add thinly sliced red onion and finely chopped jalapeño pepper. 3. Combine lime juice, lemon juice, cilantro, olive oil, salt, and pepper in a separate container. 4. Drizzle the citrus mixture over the tuna and gently toss to coat. Cover the bowl and refrigerate it for 20-30 minutes. 5. Give the ceviche a gentle toss before serving. Serve the ceviche on lettuce leaves or cucumber slices.

NUTRIENTS (PER SERVINGS)

Cholesterol: 30mg | Sodium: 100mg | Carbs: 7g | Fiber: 1g | Sugar: 2g | Protein: 20g

3. OPEN SARDINE SANDWICH

Servings: 2   Duration: 10 minutes

INGREDIENTS	INSTRUCTIONS
<ul><li>1 can of sardines in water or olive oil (no added sugars)</li><li>1 small avocado, sliced.</li><li>Fresh spinach leaves</li><li>1 tomato, sliced.</li><li>Lemon juice, salt, and pepper to taste</li><li>1/4 red onion, sliced.</li><li>4 slices of whole-grain bread</li></ul>	1. Drain the sardines and use a fork to separate them. 2. In a small bowl, squeeze fresh lemon juice over the sardines and season with salt and pepper to taste. Mix well. 3. Toast slices whole grain bread. 4. Apply a layer of sliced avocado on the bread and top each slice with a layer of spinach leaves. 5. Place the tomato slices on top of the spinach leaves. Add a portion of the seasoned sardines to each slice. 6. Place the seasoned sardines and red onion slices on top. 7. Serve the dish and savor the flavors!

NUTRIENTS (PER SERVINGS)

Carbs: 25g | Protein: 14g | Fat: 13g | Fiber: 8g

4. HUMMUS

Servings: 6   Duration: 10 minutes

INGREDIENTS	INSTRUCTIONS
<ul><li>2 cups canned chickpeas drained and rinsed.</li><li>2 garlic cloves, minced.</li><li>1/4 cup tahini</li><li>1/2 tsp ground cumin</li><li>1/4 tsp salt (optional)</li><li>2 tbsp extra-virgin olive oil</li><li>2-4 tbsp water (as needed)</li><li>1 tbsp chopped fresh parsley (for garnish)</li><li>2 tbsp fresh lemon juice</li></ul>	1. Combine chickpeas, tahini, olive oil, lemon juice, minced garlic, cumin, and salt in a blender and blend until the mixture becomes smooth. 2. Gradually add water to achieve the desired thickness. 3. Taste and adjust the seasoning as needed. 4. Move the mixture to a serving bowl, decorate with parsley, and savor!

NUTRIENTS (PER SERVINGS)

Carbohydrates: 12g | Fiber: 4g | Sugars: 1g | Protein: 5g

5. FRESH DILL DIP

Servings: 8   Duration: 10 minutes

INGREDIENTS	INSTRUCTIONS
• 1 cup plain Greek yogurt. • 1 tbsp freshly squeezed lemon juice • 1 clove garlic, minced. • 1/4 cup light sour cream • Salt and pepper to taste • 2 tbsp freshly chopped dill • 1 tbsp freshly squeezed lemon juice	1. Combine Greek yogurt and low-fat sour cream in a mixing bowl. 2. Add minced garlic, dill, lemon juice, salt, and pepper. 3. Mix well to ensure all ingredients are well blended. 4. Cover the bowl and place it in the refrigerator for half an hour. Enjoy the dip alongside a selection of fresh vegetables.

NUTRIENTS (PER SERVINGS)

Carbs: 2g | Fiber: 0g | Sugars: 1g | Protein: 4g | Cholesterol: 5mg

6. CREAMY CHEESE DIP

Servings: 6   Duration: 15 minutes

INGREDIENTS	INSTRUCTIONS
• 1/4 tsp dried dill • 2 cloves garlic, minced. • 1 tbsp fresh lemon juice • 1 cup plain Greek yogurt (low-fat) • 1/4 tsp black pepper • 1 cup reduced-fat cream cheese. • 1/4 tsp paprika • Fresh parsley or chives (optional) • 1/4 tsp onion powder • 1 cup shredded reduced-fat cheddar cheese. • Assorted fresh vegetables for dipping	1. Combine cream cheese, Greek yogurt, cheddar cheese, lemon juice, black pepper, paprika, onion powder, and dried dill. 2. Warm the mixture over low heat until it becomes melted and smooth. 3. Allow it to cool a bit, and then transfer it to a bowl for serving. 4. Sprinkle fresh parsley or chives on top for decoration. 5. Serve alongside fresh vegetables to dip into the mixture.

NUTRIENTS (PER SERVINGS)

Carbs: 5g | Protein: 10g | Fat: 7g | Fiber: 1g | Sugar: 3g

7. SPINACH AND ARTICHOKE DIP

Servings: 6   Duration: 30 minutes

INGREDIENTS	INSTRUCTIONS
• 1 cup canned artichoke hearts drained and chopped. • 1/2 cup plain Greek yogurt (low-fat) • 1/4 cup shredded mozzarella cheese (part-skim) • 1/2 cup light cream cheese • 2 cloves garlic, minced. • 1/2 tsp onion powder • 1/4 tsp black pepper • 1/4 cup grated Parmesan cheese. • 1/4 tsp salt • 1 cup frozen spinach, thawed and drained	1. Preheat the oven to 350°F (175°C). 2. Combine spinach, artichoke hearts, Greek yogurt, cream cheese, Parmesan cheese, mozzarella cheese, garlic, onion powder, black pepper, and salt in a bowl. 3. Transfer the mixture to a baking dish coated with cooking spray. 4. Bake for approximately 20 minutes until the dish is heated through. 5. Serve warm with vegetable sticks or whole-grain crackers.

NUTRIENTS (PER SERVINGS)

Carbs: 7g | Protein: 8g | Fat: 6g | Fiber: 3g | Sodium: 323mg | Sugar: 2g

8. NO-BAKE COCONUT AND CASHEW ENERGY BARS

Servings: 10   Duration: 30 minutes

INGREDIENTS	INSTRUCTIONS
• 1/4 cup almond flour • 1 tbsp powdered, low-calorie sweetener • 1/4 cup unsweetened almond butter • 2 tbsp unsweetened cocoa powder • 1/4 cup coconut oil, melted. • 1 cup unsweetened shredded coconut • 1 tsp vanilla extract • 1 cup raw cashews • Pinch of salt	1. Put the almond flour, cocoa powder, coconut, cashews, low-calorie sweetener, and salt in a food processor. Blend the mixture well. 2. Next, add almond butter, melted coconut oil, and 3. vanilla extract to the mixture. Blend until a sticky dough is formed. 4. Press dough into a line baking dish. Place the dish in the re-frigerator and let it chill for at least 1 hour. 5. Cut into bars and store in an airtight container in the fridge.

NUTRIENTS (PER SERVINGS)

Carbs: 7g | Fiber: 3g | Sugars: 2g | Protein: 4g | Sodium: 20mg

. CINNAMON TOASTED PUMPKIN SEEDS

Servings: 8   Duration: 30 minutes

INGREDIENTS	INSTRUCTIONS
• 1 tbsp melted coconut oil • 1/4 tsp salt • 1 tbsp sugar substitute • 2 cups pumpkin seeds • 1 tsp ground cinnamon	1. Preheat the oven to 325°F (163°C). 2. Combine coconut oil, sugar substitute, cinnamon, and salt in a bowl. 3. Coat the pumpkin seeds with the mixture. Spread the seeds on a baking sheet lined with parchment paper. 4. Bake for 15-20 min until they turn golden and crispy, stirring halfway through. 5. Let it cool before serving.

NUTRIENTS (PER SERVINGS)

Carbs: 4g | Fiber: 2g | Carbs: 2g | Fat: 12g | Protein: 8g

0. CUCUMBER PATE

Servings: 4   Duration: 15 minutes

INGREDIENTS	INSTRUCTIONS
• 2 medium-sized cucumbers • 2 cloves garlic, minced. • 2 tbsp fresh dill, chopped. • 1/2 cup plain Greek yogurt. • 2 tbsp fresh lemon juice • Salt and pepper to taste	1. Peel and grate the cucumbers by excluding seeds and remove any extra moisture. 2. Combine the grated cucumber with garlic, dill, Greek yogurt, and lemon juice. 3. Add salt and pepper to taste. 4. Allow the mixture to cool in the refrigerator for one hour. Serve the mixture as a spread or dip.

NUTRIENTS (PER SERVINGS)

Carbs: 6g | Fiber: 1g | Protein: 5g | Fat: 2g | Sodium: 50mg

CHAPTER 12

DESSERTS

1. Fried Apples

2. Strawberry Cream Cheese Crepes

3. Raspberry Nice Cream

4. Cherry Almond Cobbler

5. Basic Pie Crust

6. Crustless Peanut Butter Cheesecake

7. Lemon Dessert Shots

8. Chocolate Cupcakes

9. Pumpkin Spice Waffles

10. Blueberry Yogurt Cake

. FRIED APPLES

Servings: 4   Duration: 20 minutes

INGREDIENTS	INSTRUCTIONS
• 1 tbsp coconut oil • 4 medium-sized apples (low glycemic index) • 1/2 tsp nutmeg • 1 tbsp unsalted butter • 1 tbsp lemon juice • Stevia (optional) • 1 tsp cinnamon	1. Peel and slice the apples. 2. Heat a skillet and melt butter and coconut oil. 3. Place the apple slices in the skillet coated with the melted butter and oil. 4. Sprinkle cinnamon and nutmeg over the apple slices. 5. Squeeze some lemon juice to prevent turning brown. Stir occasionally. 6. Cook for 10-12 minutes until tender and caramelized. 7. Serve alone or as a topping.

NUTRIENTS (PER SERVINGS)

Carbs: 20g | Fiber: 5g | Fat: 5g | Protein: 1g

. STRAWBERRY CREAM CHEESE CREPES

Servings: 4   Duration: 35 minutes

INGREDIENTS	INSTRUCTIONS
• 1 cup whole wheat flour • 2 cups fresh strawberries, sliced. • 1 tbsp sugar substitute • Cooking spray • 1/2 tsp baking powder • 1/4 tsp salt • 2 large eggs • 1 cup unsweetened almond milk • 1 tbsp sugar substitute • 1 tbsp lemon juice • 1 tsp vanilla extract (optional) 4 oz reduced-fat cream cheese. 1 tbsp sugar substitute	1. Whisk flour, sugar substitute, baking powder, and salt. 2. In another bowl, whisk almond milk, eggs, and vanilla extract. 3. Blend the wet and dry ingredients, whisking until the mixture becomes smooth. 4. Warm up a skillet, apply cooking spray to coat it, and pour 1/4 cup of batter to create thin crepes. 5. Cook each crepe on each side for 1-2 minutes, then transfer them to a plate. 6. Combine cream cheese, sugar substitute, and vanilla extract until smooth. 7. In another bowl, mix strawberries, sugar substitutes, and lemon juice. 8. Spread the cream cheese filling on each crepe and roll them up. 9. Add the strawberry mixture on top. Serve and enjoy!

NUTRIENTS (PER SERVINGS)

Carbs: 25g | Protein: 9g | Fat: 9g | Fiber: 4g | Sugar: 6g

3. RASPBERRY NICE CREAM

Servings: 5   Duration: 2-3 hours

INGREDIENTS	INSTRUCTIONS
<ul><li>2 cups frozen raspberries</li><li>1 tsp vanilla extract</li><li>2 medium-sized ripe bananas, frozen and sliced.</li><li>1/2 cup unsweetened almond milk</li></ul>	1. Combine frozen raspberries, frozen bananas, almond milk, and vanilla extract in a blender until the mixture becomes smooth. 2. Add low-calorie sweeteners like stevia, honey, or maple syrup to adjust the sweetness if desired. 3. Transfer the mixture to a freezer-safe container, smooth the top, and cover. 4. Freeze for approx. 2-3 hours until firm. 5. Before serving, let it soften a bit, then scoop it into bowls and add any desired garnishes.

NUTRIENTS (PER SERVINGS)

Carbs: 20g | Fiber: 5g | Sugars: 8g | Protein: 1g | Sodium: 30mg

4. CHERRY ALMOND COBBLER

Servings: 6   Duration: 30 minutes

INGREDIENTS	INSTRUCTIONS
<ul><li>4 cups pitted cherries.</li><li>1 tbsp lemon juice</li><li>1 cup almond flour</li><li>1/2 tsp cinnamon</li><li>1/4 cup rolled oats.</li><li>2 tbsp melted unsalted butter or coconut oil.</li><li>1/4 cup chopped almonds.</li><li>1/2 tsp almond extract</li><li>1/4 cup sugar substitute</li><li>Pinch of salt</li></ul>	1. Preheat the oven to 350°F (175°C). 2. Combine cherries with lemon juice and a sugar substitute. Allow them to rest for 10 minutes. 3. Mix almond flour, oats, almonds, butter, almond extract, cinnamon, and salt in a separate bowl. 4. Place the cherry mixture in a baking dish. 5. Sprinkle the almond flour mixture over the cherries. 6. Bake for approximately 30 minutes until the dish turns golden and bubbles. 7. Allow it to cool slightly before serving. 8. Serve it with sugar-free vanilla ice cream or whipped cream. (Optional)

NUTRIENTS (PER SERVINGS)

Carbohydrates: 12g | Fiber: 3g | Protein: 5g | Sodium: 20mg | Potassium: 250mg | Sugar: 5g

5. BASIC PIE CRUST

Servings: 8   Duration: 30 minutes

INGREDIENTS	INSTRUCTIONS
<ul><li>1 ¼ cups almond flour</li><li>2 tbsp unsalted butter, melted.</li><li>¼ cup coconut flour</li><li>2 tbsp ground flaxseed</li><li>1 large egg</li><li>¼ tsp salt</li></ul>	1. Preheat oven to 350°F (175°C). 2. Combine coconut flour, almond flour, flaxseed, and salt in a bowl. 3. Add melted butter and an egg to the dry ingredients and mix until the dough is formed. 4. Press the dough evenly along the bottom and sides of the pan, forming the crust. 5. Use a fork to create tiny holes in the bottom of the crust. 6. Bake at 350°F for 10-12 minutes or until the crust turns golden brown. 7. Let the crust cool completely before filling.

NUTRIENTS (PER SERVINGS)

Carbs: 8g | Fiber: 4g | Carbs: 4g | Protein: 6g | Fat: 14g

6. CRUSTLESS PEANUT BUTTER CHEESECAKE

Servings: 8-10   Duration: 45 minutes   Chilling Time: 4 hours or overnight

INGREDIENTS	INSTRUCTIONS
<ul><li>16 oz (450g) cream cheese, softened.</li><li>Chopped peanuts (optional)</li><li>1/2 cup (120g) natural peanut butter</li><li>Sugar-free whipped cream (optional)</li><li>1/2 cup (120ml) unsweetened almond milk</li><li>2 large eggs</li><li>1/2 cup (120g) granulated sugar substitute.</li><li>1 tsp vanilla extract</li></ul>	1. Preheat the oven to 325°F (160°C) and apply a thin layer of butter to a 9-inch (23cm) cake pan. 2. Add peanut butter, almond milk, creamed cheese, 1/4 cup of sugar substitute, and vanilla in a mixing bowl. Stir until smooth. 3. Add the eggs one by one, mixing well after each addition. 4. Taste the batter and adjust the sweetness. Then, pour the batter into the greased cake pan. 5. Bake for 45-50 minutes or until the center of the cake is firm. 6. Allow the cake to cool for one hour, then place it in the refrigerator for at least four hours or overnight. 7. Top it with sugar-free whipped cream and chopped peanuts. Serve!

NUTRIENTS (PER SERVINGS)

Carbs: 4g | Fiber: 1g | Sugars: 1g | Protein: 8g

7. LEMON DESSERT SHOTS

Servings: 4   Duration: 15 minutes

INGREDIENTS	INSTRUCTIONS
• 1 cup Greek yogurt, un-sweetened • 1 tbsp lemon zest • 2 tbsp powdered sugar substitute • 1/2 cup crushed sugar-free graham crackers • 1 tsp vanilla extract • 1/4 cup freshly squeezed lemon juice	1. Combine lemon juice, lemon zest, Greek yogurt, powdered sugar alternative, and vanilla extract in a bowl. 2. Place crushed sugar-free graham crackers as the base in dessert glasses. 3. Now add a spoonful of the lemon yogurt mixture over the graham cracker layer. 4. Continue layering until all the ingredients are utilized. 5. Place a dollop of lemon yogurt mixture on top and garnish with remaining raspberries. 6. Chill and let it set in the refrigerator for at least 60 minutes. 7. Serve cold and savor!

NUTRIENTS (PER SERVINGS)

Carbohydrates: 7g | Fiber: 1g | Net Carbohydrates: 6g | Protein: 6g | Fat: 3g

8. CHOCOLATE CUPCAKES

Servings: 2   Duration: 20 minutes

INGREDIENTS	INSTRUCTIONS
• 1 cup almond flour • 1/4 cup unsweetened apple-sauce • 1/2 tsp baking powder • 1/4 cup unsalted butter, melted. • 1/2 cup unsweetened al-mond milk • 1/4 cup granulated sweeten-er • 2 large eggs • 1/2 cup unsweetened cocoa powder • 1 tsp vanilla extract • 1/4 tsp salt	1. Preheat your oven to 350°F (175°C) and line a cupcake pans. 2. Combine almond flour, baking powder, cocoa powder, and salt in a bowl. Mix them together. 3. In another bowl, combine melted butter, applesauce, and sweeten-er. 4. Add the eggs one at a time and stir in the vanilla extract. 5. Gradually add the dry ingredients to the wet mixture, alternating with almond milk. 6. Fill the cupcake liners about 2/3 full and bake for 18-20 min approx. 7. Allow the cupcakes to cool on a wire rack before optionally adding frosting. 8. For frosting: Beat cream cheese, sweetener, and vanilla extract until the mixture is smooth. Frost the cupcakes and enjoy!

NUTRIENTS (PER SERVINGS)

Carbs: 8g | Dietary Fiber: 4g | Sugars: 1g | Protein: 5g | Sodium: 85mg

. PUMPKIN SPICE WAFFLES

Servings: 4   Duration: 30 minutes

INGREDIENTS	INSTRUCTIONS
• 1 cup whole wheat flour • 1/2 tsp baking soda • 1 tsp cinnamon • 1/2 cup unsweetened almond milk • 1/2 tsp ginger • 1/4 tsp salt • 1 cup canned pumpkin puree. • Cooking spray • 2 tsp baking powder • 1/4 cup unsweetened applesauce • 1/2 cup almond flour • 2 tbsp sugar-free maple syrup • 1 tsp vanilla extract • 1/4 tsp nutmeg	1. Preheat the waffle iron. 2. Blend almond flour, baking soda, ginger, nutmeg, salt, whole wheat flour, baking powder, and cinnamon. 3. in a bowl. 4. Combine maple syrup, almond milk, applesauce, pumpkin puree, and vanilla extract in a separate bowl. 5. Pour the wet mixture into the dry ingredients and stir until just mixed. 6. Lightly coat the waffle iron with cooking spray. 7. Pour the batter onto the preheated waffle iron and cook for 4-6 minutes, until golden brown. 8. Repeat the process with the remaining batter. 9. Serve the waffles warm with sugar-free maple syrup.

NUTRIENTS (PER SERVINGS)

Carbs: 27g | Protein: 7g | Fat: 7g | Sodium: 400mg | Sugar: 4g

0. BLUEBERRY YOGURT CAKE

Servings: 6   Duration: 50 minutes

INGREDIENTS	INSTRUCTIONS
• 1 cup almond flour • 3/4 cup fresh or frozen blueberries • 1/4 cup coconut flour • 1 1/2 tsp baking powder • 1/4 cup honey or sugar substitute • 1/4 cup unsweetened applesauce • 1/4 tsp baking soda • 1/8 tsp salt • 2 large eggs • 3/4 cup plain Greek yogurt. • 1/2 tsp vanilla extract	1. Preheat the oven to 350°F (175°C) and grease a 6-inch round cake pan. 2. Combine almond flour, coconut flour, baking powder, baking soda, and salt in a bowl. 3. Mix Greek yogurt, eggs, applesauce, honey, and vanilla extract in another bowl. 4. Gradually add the dry ingredients to the wet ingredients and stir until combined. Now add blueberries to the mixture. Stir gently. 5. Pour the batter into the greased cake pan, spreading it evenly. 6. Bake for 35-40 minutes or until a toothpick inserted comes out clean. Remove from oven, transfer it to a wire rack to cool completely. Dust with powdered sugar substitute before serving. (optional)

NUTRIENTS (PER SERVINGS)

Carbs: 14g | Fiber: 3g | Fat: 2g | Protein: 9g | Sugar: 7g

INDEX: 30-DAY MEAL PLAN

B = Breakfast, L = Lunch, D = Dinner, S = Sn

n this "**30-day meal plan**" section, you'll find various delectable recipes designed specifical-y with diabetes management in mind. From breakfast to dinner and even snacks, these dishes are deli-ious and carefully crafted to keep your blood sugar levels in check. With this meal plan, you'll find that nourishing your body and soul is a delightful journey you'll never want to end.

Ready to manage your diabetes? Read on!

DAY 1		DAY 2	
B	Vegetable Omelette with Spinach, mush-rooms	B	Overnight oats with unsweetened almond milk
L	Grilled Chicken Salad	L	Turkey Wrap with Whole Wheat Tortilla
D	Baked Salmon with roasted asparagus and quinoa	D	Lean Beef Stir-Fry with Broccoli
		S	Greek yogurt with berries

DAY 3		DAY 4	
B	Greek yogurt parfait	B	Pumpkin Spice Muffins
L	Turkey & Rice Soup	L	Mustard Herb Pork Tenderloin
D	Tuna and white bean salad	D	Baked cod with roasted Brussels sprouts

DAY 5		DAY 6	
B	Almond Berry Oatmeal	B	Cauliflower Scramble
L	Baked Turkey Spaghetti	L	Crispy Chicken Thighs
D	Creamy Broccoli Soup	D	Catfish with Corn and Pepper Rel-ish
S	Hard-boiled eggs with a sprinkle of sea salt		

DAY 7		DAY 8	
B	Unsweetened Lemonad Milk, Spin-ach, Banana Smoothie	B	Cheesy Scrambled Eggs
L	Steak Gyro Platter	L	Teriyaki Turkey Meatballs
D	Lentil and vegetable soup	D	Trout with Basil Sauce
		S	Cottage Cheese With Sliced Peache

DAY 9		DAY 10	
B	Veggie scramble with eggs	B	Whole grain toast topped with av-ocado.
L	Blackened Salmon	L	Jalapeno Popper Pork Chops
D	Bavarian Beef	D	Cheddar-Beef Burger

DAY 7		DAY 8	
B	Banana Pancakes	B	Breakfast Burrito
L	Nut butter rollup, berries	L	Lemony Kale Salad
D	Chicken masala	D	Lamb Shanks & Grilled Vegetables
	Cinnamon Toasted Pumpkin Seeds	S	Spinach and Artichoke Dip

DAY 11		DAY 22	
B	Healthy Granola	B	Seedy Muesli
L	Quinoa and black bean	L	Chicken Pot Pie
D	Grilled Lean Steak with Roasted Sweet potato	D	Butternut Squash Soup

DAY 13		DAY 14	
B	Veggie and cheese omelet	B	Egg muffins
L	Beef Stroganoff	L	Sole Piccata
D	Thanksgiving Turkey Breast	D	White Bean Soup
		S	Celery Sticks with Peanut Butter

DAY 15		DAY 16	
B	Egg-Stuffed Tomatoes	B	Asparagus Frittata
L	Spinach and mushroom quesadilla	L	Grilled Pork Loin Chops
D	Aromatic Mackerel	D	Caprese Shrimp Pasta

DAY 17		DAY 18	
B	Pita pizza	B	Banana Smoothie
L	Tuna Poke with Riced Broccoli	L	Baked Cod with Tomatoes and Olives
D	Lemon-Garlic Mushrooms	D	Stuffed Bell peppers
S	Almonds and dried apricots		

DAY 19		DAY 20	
B	Basic Pie Crust	B	Blueberry nut balls
L	Chicken Nuggets	L	Feta Spinach Salad
D	Steak rolls creamed spinach	D	Cod with Mango Salsa
		S	Fennel and Chickpeas

DAY 21			DAY 22	
B	Banana Pancakes		B	Breakfast Burrito
L	Nut butter rollup, berries		L	Lemony Kale Salad
D	Chicken masala		D	Lamb Shanks & Grilled Vegetables
S	Cinnamon Toasted Pumpkin Seeds		S	Spinach and Artichoke Dip
DAY 23			**DAY 24**	
B	Poached eggs		B	Hard-boiled eggs and Sliders
L	Bell pepper Sandwich		L	Fried Rice
D	Grilled Halibut		D	Stuffed Chicken Breast
DAY 25			**DAY 26**	
B	Biscuits & Gravy		B	Oats with Blueberry toppings
L	Apple-Carrot salad		L	Spinach Tomato Tart
D	Pork Chop Diane		D	Chicken Salad
S	Carrot sticks with hummus			
DAY 27			**DAY 28**	
B	Pumpkin Porridge		B	Crustless Quiche
L	Sausage Sammies		L	Feta Spinach Salad
D	Shredded Buffalo Chicken		D	Beef steaks
			S	Cucumber Pate
DAY 29			**DAY 30**	
B	Strawberry Cream Cheese Crepes		B	Yogurt & Granola
L	Broccoli with Pine Nuts		L	Lemon Chicken Breast
D	Open Sardine Sandwich		D	Beef Brisket
S	Parmesan Zucchini Fries			

CONCLUSION

In conclusion, this Diabetic Diet Cookbook is an invaluable resource for individuals with diabetes who are seeking to manage their condition effectively through diet and lifestyle choices. Throughout this book, we have provided comprehensive information on diabetes including its causes, symptoms, and complications, while emphasizing the importance of a balanced and controlled diet in maintaining optimal blood sugar levels.

The recipes in this cookbook are carefully crafted to meet the specific dietary needs of individuals with diabetes. They are designed to be delicious, nutritious, and easy to prepare, ensuring that individuals can enjoy various flavors and dishes while adhering to their dietary requirements. We have prioritized ingredients low in sugar, carbohydrates, and unhealthy fats, while also focusing on incorporating nutrient-rich foods that can support overall health and well-being.

Embracing a diabetic diet is not about deprivation or sacrificing taste; it is about making informed choices and taking control of one's health. By following the guidelines and recipes in this cookbook individuals can manage their blood sugar levels effectively, reduce the risk of complications, and improve their overall quality of life.

We encourage you to embark on this journey towards a healthier lifestyle by incorporating these recipes into your daily routine. Small changes in your diet can significantly impact your well-being and long-term health. We are confident that with the right knowledge and support, you can achieve your health goals and enjoy a fulfilling life with diabetes.

Remember, you have the power to take control of your health, and we are honored to be part of your journey toward a happier and healthier future.

But hold onto your aprons, for the feast does not end here! Explore our other two sensational cookbooks "DASH Diet for Beginners" and "Renal Diet for Beginners" - crafted with the same passion and expertise as this one.

We invite you to spread joy and inspire others on their diabetes management journey.

As authors, it brings us great joy to know that our work has resonated with readers like you and has the potential to impact your life positively. Your support and dedication to managing your diabetes are truly inspiring.

WE APPRECIATE YOUR TIME, EFFORT, AND ENTHUSIASM!

PLEASE TAKE A FEW MINUTES TO SHARE YOUR EXPERIENCE BY LEAVING A
REVIEW ON AMAZON.

Yours truly,

Emily

Made in the USA
Las Vegas, NV
04 November 2023

80174473R00057